ANNETTE CHARPENTIER

FEAR –

THE COMPLETE GUIDE TO GETTING THROUGH IT

Distributed by:
United Kingdom
Airlift Book Company
8 The Arena, Mollison Avenue,
Enfield, Middlesex EN3 7NJ
London

USA
Midpoint Trade Books
27 West 20th Street,
New York NY 10011-3707

Australia
Tower Books
PO Box 213
Brookvale, NSW 2100

Publisher/Producer: Fiaz Rafiq

Published by: HNL Publishing, Suite 185, 6 Wilmslow Road, Manchester M14 5TP, United Kingdom

e-mail: hnlpub@hotmail.com
ISBN: 0953176681

© 2005 Annette Charpentier
All rights reserved. No part of this publication may be reproduced or stored in a retrieval system or transmitted in any form or by any means electronic, mechanical, recording or otherwise without the prior written permission of the publisher

Acknowledgements

I would like to thank my publisher for letting me get on with the subject in my own way and for giving me time. I would also like to thank my extended family for exactly the same things – for letting me get on with the book and giving me all their support and time.
I hope we didn't lose too much precious time of togetherness.

Disclaimer

The cases cited in this book are not based on real people. Some client material has been used but altered and adapted for reasons of confidentiality and readability

The author and the publisher can't take any responsibility for any effects the book might have on readers.

Contents

Foreword — *page 11*

"Fear Makes the Heart Sink"
– an Introduction — *page 12*

Part I:
"Fear Sickens the Soul" — *page 27*
– The Latest Research on the Physical Facts underlying Fear and Panic

Part II
"When I Look up at the Stars, I feel Giddy" — *page 73*
– Alone with Yourself

Part III
"There is no Fear without Hope and no Hope without Fear" — *page 101*
– Fear and Control
– Do's and Don'ts

Afterword: Embrace your Fear — *page 152*

Bibliography — *page 154*

Foreword

It has been a fascinating journey, researching for this book on fear – our old companion, one of the strongest negative emotions we know, the driving force for many, many unpleasant but also very constructive life events. Most people I shared my plan with responded similarly: "Wow! That sounds interesting!"

Fear makes us shake. "No passion so effectually robs the mind of all its powers of acting and reasoning as fear" (Edmund Burke) – but somehow we take it for granted, and don't ask what exactly happens to us when we experience it, what it triggers, what choices we have and how much control we can exercise to keep its exaggerated form under control. We seldom ponder of how closely connected fear is with the way we fundamentally feel about ourselves – that fear in one form or the other is actually at the heart of our human existence. Life is not, like the English poet Larkin put it, "first boredom and then fear" – fear is and has been with us all the time. Some people are called fearless, and we admire them. But is it really such a good idea to strive for a life apparently without any fear? What about dangers, what about risks – what about the thrill we get from watching scary movies, when we go on risky adventures or pursue extreme sports?

It's what we do with fear and what it does with us - that's what we would like to throw a light on in this book. Looking at fear in a broader, evolutionary context and drawing practical conclusions from this maybe will help a few people to change the debilitating effect fear has on them. The aim is not to live a life without fear. It's about getting to know it better and to integrate it into your life by taking control of this, in my mind our strongest emotion.

"Fear Makes the Heart Sink" – an Introduction

There is not a single human being on this planet who would not know what we mean by fear– that sinking feeling, the dread forming a tight knot in the pit of our stomach, the heart starting to pound, until we hear it ringing in our ears. First our palms begin to sweat, then the rest of the body. We feel utterly tense and at the same time frozen, paralysed. Our thoughts are either racing through all the possible options for response, or the mind goes blank and numb.

Only Six Emotions

We are talking about one of our six basic emotions as Darwin defined them – the others being anger, sadness, pleasure/happiness, disgust and surprise. Yes, there are more than that, each of those six having a spectrum of more subtle, specific feelings. With surprise for example, it ranges from being mildly startled to thrilling excitement. Sadness can be said to reach from feeling a little low to heart-wrenching grief. But as broad categories of basic emotions, we can make do with just six.

The Oldest Companion

Among these, fear is probably our oldest companion. Most likely, it has not only been with us since our human minds evolved, but from long before that, going back to primate life and beyond. Some trace the emotion of fear back to primeval fish. As such an old feeling, we share it with most animals. Though we don't know what is going on in the mind of a rat being stared at by a rattlesnake, we can detect some of the same physical signs – frozenness, trembling and pilo-erection (the raising of the body hair, which humans feel on the head and neck).

One could call fear our best survival mechanism ever. Without fear we would have rushed into dangerous situations aeons ago - and would have perished as a species. Without fear of some imagined future situation, we would have forgone all planning with the aim to avoid it, and maybe have dwindled away as a race, forever caught out on the wrong foot. Without fear as a driving force and a companion of risky but important undertakings, we would have stayed put on our trees or in our caves.

Two Sides of the Coin

So, as devastating an emotion as it can be, fear has the potential flip-side of propelling us forward and making us and our lives safer as individuals and as a species. Yet, when we mention fear, this avenue it can take is almost always forgotten. Our first and all subsequent associations with fear are entirely negative. Fear is what we definitely don't want to feel. Fear is what we strive to avoid. We do not want to experience the sensations described above. And yet many people suffer from one or the other, or most of its elements in a crippling way day in day out, triggered by all sorts of real, unreal or perceived dangers.

"I can't do this!"

Speaking in public is one of the most mentioned situations that people describe as "scary". Lots of us know the slow build up of all the horrible physical reactions following the thought: "In five minutes from now I will have to stand up and say something in front of all these people!" But then, when the moment comes, most people manage to do just that. They start, and the sense of imminent danger vanishes the moment the thoughts focus on what we have or want to say. However, the effect of the adrenaline rush caused by negative anticipation (or fear) remains, resulting in total alertness. Our voice is a bit croaky at the beginning, but after clearing it, we can actually perform well – and probably, what with that adrenaline rush, even better than if we had been perfectly cool and calm.

Other situations commonly associated with fear are heights: when we are standing on the edge of a precipice, be it on a first floor balcony, in a ski-lift, on a mountain ridge, in an aeroplane – or in the slightly higher seat of a people carrier driving down the motorway. In all those situations, when we suffer from fear of heights, the body's responses are the same, because the triggered emotion is the same: It feels near enough intolerable.
And yet, we do it, and very often experiences accompanied by the "fear syndrome" stick much clearer in our memory either to haunt us, or to make better sense of a situation.

All Kinds of Fear

In this book, we want to explore the mechanism of this strong emotion and trace all the thoughts, physical sensations, feelings and behaviour patterns connected with it in order to tell which one is which. Which one of our fears is real and has to be followed by appropriate action? Which ones are unreal and triggered either by some chemical-electrical process in our brain gone haywire or by an old fear memory that has been imprinted in our unconscious brain indelibly? And which ones of our fears are only perceived, meaning that our appraisal of a certain situation is distorted, triggering a response that is then wholly inappropriate and dangerous?

Latest Research

Based on latest research, we will trace the neural pathways that fear takes from the external trigger to the various processing centres in the brain down to the last tiny nerve fibre in our fingertips.

Based on that knowledge, we can make suggestions about how to deal with this dreaded and dreadful emotion, when we are gripped by it out of proportion, when our day to day life is not only influenced by it, but crippled. When our behaviour is shaped by it, and with it our social life, our work life – in short, everything.

So we all know fear, and we can distinguish different kinds of real fear in really dangerous situations. We will identify perceived fear, when we only think a situation is dangerous, and explore the fear "out of the blue", often called panic, or even panic attack, when it crushes down on us unexpectedly.

Existential Fear

Most people are also familiar with yet another kind of fear, not a kind of "fear of…" something external, but rather an anxiety from within, a feeling of dread when faced with the precariousness of human existence and of ultimately being all alone. Philosophers have dealt with this in past and present, coming to various conclusions. They agree, however, on the universality of this existential fear. It has to do with who and where we are on this planet, a pinprick in an infinite universe. The chapter "Alone with Yourself" will deal with some aspects of this kind of fear and with ways to cope with it.

Put the Fear on a Leash
So far, the one and only way to come to grips with panic attacks out of the blue, with that dreadful fear out of control, was by adopting the principles of cognitive-behavioural therapy. This meant, picking apart the process of fear into chunks of different processes, based on the theory that our thinking influences how we feel, which in turn has certain physical responses as a consequence, which in turn result in a particular behaviour. Victims of fear are taught to pinpoint their "hot negative thoughts". Hot negative thoughts are conscious or half-conscious messages going through our head which trigger a negative feeling response and the accompanying physical sensations, and result in undesirable or downright bizarre behaviour. For example, a message at the back of our mind saying "You're not good enough. How can anybody possibly like me?" triggers feelings of insecurity, fear of rejection, timidity and anxiety. These feelings are accompanied by symptoms of nervousness such as blushing, sweating, and maybe trembling. The behaviour following these feelings and physical reactions is most likely withdrawal from situations which trigger this kind of response, which results in a kind of social phobia – based on the fear of what might happen when we expose our unvalued selves to other people's judgment.

Find the "Hot Thought"
Cognitive behavioural therapy will focus on the thought element of this vicious cycle. If we manage to alter the old message "Nobody likes me" by exploring it rationally and searching for evidence for and against it, we will, by and by, be able to break its power to cause the unpleasant feelings and the undesired behaviour

This cognitive behavioural approach of managing fear is very successful – but not for everybody. We will show in this book why the cognitive approach, the breaking of the cycle of fear at the point of "thought", in the realm of rational thinking, does not and cannot always work, because according to latest research the underlying bio-neurological processes are different from what we had assumed before.

Embrace the Feeling
These days we know more about the processes inside our brains than ever before. Even though we are a long way away from a complete "map" of the brain, we know a good deal more facts about what is going on "up there" than even five years ago. This enables us to rethink some of the theories held before.

Live with Your Fear
Based on new facts and insight, we will suggest a different approach. This does not mean dismissing the cognitive-behavioural approach altogether, but giving it a fundamentally different assumption: We cannot "do away" with fear by conditioning and training our brains. The goal can't be to live without fear. Fear very often is "in our bones" – not just in the sense of previous experiences of this strong feeling, having lived through risky or dangerous situations, but also as a useful, strong set of responses which serves an important purpose. For our survival and emotional balance, it is much more effective to embrace fear as our old evolutionary friend rather than treating it as an arch enemy to be eradicated.

The goal is not to live without fear

We have to take our fear on board, examine and tame it, before making it manageable and tolerable. The goal is to utilize the tremendous alerting power and energy it can give us to stand and master all sorts of situations. Without this wonderfully complex mechanism that even the smallest outside signal can trigger, we would be lost very quickly. And the physical responses, that many people find so unpleasant and downright crippling, can also be seen in a different light. After all, lots of people actually love to create the feeling of cold fear by watching horror movies and reading crime stories. They enjoy the hair at the back of their neck standing on end, the goose-bumps on arms and back. Creating these feelings consciously can actually be quite a kick – but of course, we are after all staying in control and can switch off he video or TV whenever we want and let the feelings die down, if it gets too unpleasant. Experiencing the feeling of fear in this way can serve as a confirmation to us that we actually are very capable of dealing with all sorts of risky and downright dangerous situations – being, as humans, equipped with the most sophisticated response mechanism to such events. Knowing that these responses are in place and working can actually make us feel safer allround. Also, we wouldn't be capable of this complex set of physical and emotional responses without a good reason.

Embrace your fear and its tremendous energy

Throughout this book, we will follow three stories of how fear manifests itself - whether it be real, unreal or perceived, and how one can come to grips with it by accepting it, "taming" it so to say. Woven into these stories will be tips and advice about how to do this, which at the end will be presented in a simple table of Dos – and a few Don'ts.

To stay on the positive side of things, the underlying message throughout will be that it is totally in our power to tackle fear.

It is in our power to tackle fear

Three Stories

Let's begin with our three stories – stories of people suffering from fear – one from a real fear, one from a perceived one, and one about an unreal one. The stories have been simplified for better readability and by no means represent fully researched case studies. They are partly based on real people with real fears – but have been adapted for reasons of practicability and anonymity.

Fran's Story

Meet Francesca. Fran, as her friends call her, is newly married and has a 3-year-old daughter, Bibi. She and her husband Ben have been together for about four years. They are in their thirties, and both work part- time so they can share parenting Bibi.

A few years back, before Fran met Ben, she was in a four year long relationship with Tom. The relationship could be called stormy, as both were starting off on different career paths and needed different kinds of support from each other than they were able to give. So there was a lot of frustration. But that was okay, they knew how to work things out. Then, gradually, Tom's behaviour began to change. From being "ordinarily" jealous and possessive of Fran, and becoming moody and sulking whenever her work or courses took her away from home, he began to become more threatening and potentially violent when this happened – and it happened quite regularly. His personality switched dramatically from being a loving, understanding partner to a physically intimidating and confused stranger. Their life together became more and more agonizing. Before long, Tom was diagnosed with schizophrenia. He spent some time in a psychiatric unit, was put on medication to which he responded well, and was discharged.

It went well for a while, so well, that Tom forgot to take his medication more and more often. His behaviour deteriorated. One day, when Fran came home from a two-day course, he attacked her with a knife. She managed to escape, but only just. Tom was arrested, sectioned for a while, and before long was stable again on medication.

Fran, after much agonising and in spite strong feelings of guilt, told Tom that she wanted to end the relationship. As he was stable again, he consented, and promised to move away and stop contacting her. After a while, life settled down for both of them in different patterns.

Years later – Fran is now with Ben and Bibi and they are talking about another baby – she spots Tom in the High Street of her home town: Tom, who was supposed to be living a long way away down south! Her response is FEAR – a gripping feeling of her life being threatened, as it was years ago, when he attacked her with a knife. Now as then she goes through all the physical sensations described above – her heart beats fast, her mouth becomes dry, her palms are wet with sweat, her stomach becomes tight. Her fear is real. Her problem is not how to cope with her strong emotions that have an impact on every aspect of her life at that moment, but more of how to escape the situation, to reorganise her life and what steps it might take to make it safe again. Fear in her case is the aptly named "panic button" for keeping herself safe.

Gina's Story

Now let's look at Gina. Gina lives on her own during the week and works in a demanding job looking after young people in care who display challenging behaviour. She works with them on a one-to-one basis. During her working week – long two-day shifts – her entire being is focussed on the therapeutic relationship with these youngsters, who can be aggressive, violent and volatile.

At weekends, Gina's two children come to stay with her. After her divorce, she and her ex-husband had agreed that the two girls would live with their father during the week. This arrangement has proved to be the best solution for everybody involved and enables Gina to combine her challenging job with quality time with her children. It has been working out quite well for more than three years now.

In recent weeks, however, Gina has experienced sudden rushes of utter dread, of fear, of panic. Triggered by seemingly innocent situations, she is suddenly overcome by severe palpitations, her whole body starts shaking, she starts crying uncontrollably and feels utter dread. Gina is suffering from what we call panic attacks, a very common symptom of high anxiety triggered by seemingly unrelated situations. Why should she experience this "sickening of the soul", for example when she is about to cross the footbridge across the river —something she has done twice weekly for years? She has never experienced any dangerous situations in connection with it, and feels generally on top of her work and her private life.

Gina is feeling inappropriate panic, a fear unconnected to an actual life situation, an unreal fear. It does not only shake her to the core, it also utterly bewilders and confounds her, this apparent "out of the blue" attack, like a freak strike of lightning. For Gina the main priority is not to avoid a certain dangerous situation, but how to achieve a state of mind that enables her to tackle this fear and make it manageable. It is not so much about rationally trying to find a concrete reason behind it. Yes, she needs to look at possible stressors in her life, but first and foremost she needs to get a handle on the actual fear situation.

The Disco Disaster

And as a third case, let's look at the tragic incident that happened in a Chicago disco in February 2003. It was a Saturday evening and the disco, a large building with several rooms going off the main hall and numerous exits, was packed. At some point, there was an incident in front of the stage. Some people were having an argument and starting a fight. Security officers rushed in and sprayed some teargas into the knot of young people on the floor.

What happened next, was unpredictable. Even though the spraying of tear gas was not the most appropriate way of dealing with a disturbance in a closed space, the result was unforeseeable.

In the previous weeks newspaper articles and radio warnings had been alerting people to a possible chemical attack by terrorists. The general advice was to take flight at the slightest whiff of strange smells, especially "chemical" ones. If it wasn't at the forefront of people's minds, what with September 11th and the Anthrax letters a couple of months before, it was nevertheless at the back of the mind of the population as a whole. People deemed themselves under immediate threat by terrorists who would possibly resort to toxic substances to create utmost damage among civilians. This alerting, a kind of fear conditioning, had been successful. When the teargas settled and spread, a major panic set in that caused the mass of young people to blindly rush for the exits, and in the stampede, twenty-eight of them were crushed and killed. A tragic mixture of overcrowding, the steward's inappropriate use of teargas in an enclosed space, and the perceived fear of the majority of the disco-goers resulted in the tragic death of so many young people. Among other factors, it happened as a result of a wrong danger appraisal, of perceived fear.

Three different fears – and three responses with the common denominator being that our bodies and minds go out of control and allowing fear to take over our life.

The Theory so Far
So far, the following mechanism in the brain was assumed: Something is perceived by a human being through one or more of the senses (eyes, ears, nose) which is instantly recognized as "dangerous". This information is then sent along neural pathways directly to the amygdala, a small, almond-shaped part of the brain

positioned in the centre. There the "danger-signs" get processed and a certain set of responses is triggered. This results in one of three instinctive behaviour options: The body is either signalled to flee, to stand and fight, or to freeze. There are no other instinctive, non-cognitive responses to a dangerous situation, and thus the body is only programmed to these three reactions.

We have only three instinctive responses to danger: Fight, flight or freeze

Fight or Flight

In all three modes, the adrenaline production is increased. This causes the heart to beat faster and the blood to flow quicker in order to supply the muscles in the extremities with more oxygen to make them ready for either flight or fight. The increased bloodflow into the limbs draws the blood away from the brain which causes a feeling of dizziness and also an inability to think clearly (at least for a while). It also decreases the blood supply to the digestive organs (stomach and intestines) which causes the tightness in the tummy. The digestive process stops for a while. Chronically tense and anxious people often suffer from constipation as a by-product of their fearful state.

The increased heart rate also causes shortness of breath and heavier breathing to enrich the blood with more oxygen – again in preparation for physical exertion. The sweat glands increase their activity – this is maybe triggering a mechanism that goes way back, when our olfactory senses were more crucial in determining whether a situation was harmless or dangerous. When we sweat, we smell differently. We all know that frightened animals exude a different, stronger smell. So, we sweat profusely once the fear mechanism is triggered in order to warn a potential enemy by our odour that we are ready to fight.

Freeze
Sometimes this combination of hormones and physical responses causes the body (and mind) to freeze, to feel paralysed and unable to either fight or flight, until the perceived danger is over. People often report an inexplicable feeling of "total numbness" or "inability to move" in a dangerous situation. Maybe they don't even feel able to cry for help. This, too, can be traced back to a very early survival response, when hiding and being invisible would have been the best strategy. The tiger might walk past you. Just keeping still could prove a life-saver.

... and the Brain?
We all know these reactions to fearful situations, and the physical processes have been well researched and documented. What is not too well known is what is happening in the cortex, the "thinking" brain. What neural pathways are involved, how are they connected, and what exactly sets this scenario in motion when fear is triggered? Where do the danger signals go to first in the brain, and what takes priority?

In order to find the answers to these questions, we have to look precisely at what is happening in our brain. In the next part, we will unravel the complex processes of how the sensory input (the outside signals we perceive through our five senses) is processed at different stages within the brain and how the various responses are triggered.

Research of these brain processes has only just begun. Over the years, scientists have looked at some of the mechanisms triggered by external stimuli, but have only made some inroads into a full explanation of what is happening biologically, chemically, and electrically. For us, these things are important to know, because only then can we make more sense of what is happening to us when we suffer from unreal fear and panic

Outlook
We will then look at the different kinds of fear presented in our three case studies and what to do with them. Dealing with real fear is probably the easiest one, as it can be subjected to logic and analysis. It can be channelled into coping strategies and trusted, appropriate responses.

It is the unreal and perceived fear, we will concentrate on, the one that causes panic, irrational behaviour, the fear that cripples our lives and can be very stubborn, not yielding easily to rational suggestions and well thought-out strategies.

Throughout this book, we will also not forget to explore the positive role fear has to play in our lives, no matter how unpleasant it may manifest itself.

Hopefully the book leaves you with not only a broader sense of what fear, our oldest emotion, is about but also with an arsenal of methods and strategies for battling against it's crippling form, a manageable list of Dos and some Don'ts that enables us to embrace Fear and integrate it into our lives.

Part I

"Fear Sickens the Soul" – The Latest Research on the Underlying Facts of Fear and Panic*

Part I

"Fear Sickens the Soul" – The Latest Research on the Underlying Facts of Fear and Panic*

Let's have a look at precisely what is happening here. What triggers this dreadful fear mechanism? What keeps it going? Where in our bodies do we feel it?

As mentioned above, so far unreal fear and panic attacks have been tackled by a certain approach, cognitive behavioural therapy, which proves to be successful in the majority of cases of crippling fear. This theory (CBT) is based on the assumption that the cycle of fear consists of a conscious or subconscious thought which triggers a certain set of physical responses, the accompanying threatening feelings and a different, mostly unacceptable behaviour.

---

* For the information on the workings of the brain described in this chapter I am largely indebted to the book 'The Emotional Brain' by Joseph LeDoux, 1998, as well as Antonio Damasio's 'Looking for Spinoza – Joy, Sorrow and the Feeling Brain'

Fred's Story

Let's say, someone – we'll call him Fred – who has had a stormy youth, in his thirties has landed a steady job which he enjoys very much. Before that, his jobs were of the kind where not many questions were asked, where leaving one and starting another one was kind of normal. He has worked on building sites, in warehouses, as a delivery driver. This job, however, is "serious": Working as a carer with a responsibility towards a number of elderly people.

Fred loves his new job and the responsibility that goes with it. He enjoys being looked at as someone who is able to help older people with their complex needs. He feels confident and competent. He is happy to do shift-work – two days on, four days off -, which allows him to pursue his favourite outdoor pursuits, rock-climbing and canoeing, in between shifts.

Then, one day and out of the blue, while working with a group of clients, he experiences a frightening physical sensation. He thinks it's a heart attack, calls for assistance, is taken to hospital and undergoes a series of tests and examinations. To Fred's utter astonishment, the diagnosis is "panic attack". Nothing wrong with him organically. He is sent home with an explanatory leaflet that lists all the physical symptoms he has just experienced. He is confused. All he knows is that it was terrifying and that he is scared it might come back - again, just out of the blue.

For the next few weeks, Fred lives with this fear of the fear. He becomes so stressed by the thought, that he might experience another "episode", that his GP advises him to take some time off work. He also suggests some medication and/or see the counsellor.

Fred is sceptical. He never had any "mental" problems in his life before. The job is brilliant. He has always coped well. That is at least what his rational mind tells him. But his feelings say the opposite: He is scared. The fear attack has crippled him to a degree that he is now actively avoiding situations where he cannot easily escape (just in case it happens again) - like crowded rooms, trains, traffic jams...
Finally, Fred decides to see a counsellor. After a couple of session in which Fred tries to assure the counsellor that everything is fine, really, if it weren't for the continuing panic attacks. Then Fred dares to admit tentatively that he is quite nervous about losing this job. He voices vague thoughts like: "They will find out about my unsteady past", and: "If I lose this job, my whole life will be at sea".

Once these thoughts have been spoken out loud, somehow they seem to lose their power quite considerably. When they were still vague ideas, swirling around in his brain, they could upset his system from one minute to the next. Now out in the open, they seem to be kind of tamed, available for closer inspection and testing out. "What is the worst that can happen if people know that I had quite a few jobs in the past? If I really should lose this job?"

It is, as if Fred, facilitated by the counsellor, was able to retrieve from his unconscious, the "emotional" brain, some deep-seated feelings of dread, based on past experiences when jobs were lost or unsafe and practical survival was at stake. These feelings are attached to memories that often are not easily accessible, but nevertheless have a powerful impact on our consciousness, our physical well-being and on our behaviour. The memory is like an emotional appraisal of a situation which is then followed by an emotional response. And that feels different from a rational, logical appraisal which can easily be followed by a rational-logical response. Once tapped into, the emotional memory floods body and mind and locks us in the emotional state we are in.

Once out in the open, fearful thoughts can be inspected and questioned

Fred has managed to "retrieve" these old fears and bring them out for inspection and questioning. And the answers to some simple questions show that things cannot really be so bad as to justify the whole gamut of fear and survival feelings that Fred experienced when these thoughts were allowed to flood him unchecked.

Fred still experiences panic attacks, but now he is able to face them squarely. When he feels one coming on, he doesn't go to pieces any more but consciously registers the symptoms, traces the thoughts behind them and gives himself a few rational messages like: "I've experienced this before, it's not that bad, really… just wait and see, and it will go away again." With some help, he is soon able to counter the bad feelings by following some simple rules, set to scale down his frightening body reactions.

It's the Thought that Counts
We see from Fred's story that the only way to change this initially automatic response of freaking out with fear is by capturing and

defining the triggering thought, - hence "cognitive" – as we are dealing with the cognitive, the rational area of our brain.

So, in the beginning there was the word... In our case here, it is not actually the spoken word, but a mere thought, a process of the rational mind. Only that in exaggerated fear, it often is not so rational at all but a concoction of old messages going way back into childhood, of wrong assumptions and false interpretations and conclusions, which are practically indelibly imprinted on our emotional brain. That is a fact: Once something is stored in our brains, only a degenerative disease like Alzheimer's can delete it. That means, somehow or other we have to learn to live with our memories. And one way to "master" threatening memories and keep them from flooding us, is to focus on the underlying thoughts.

Memories are stored in our brains forever – consciously, unconsciously and subconsciously

---

It's a thought that triggers the chain of unpleasant events in a panic attack. What we think in any situation sets in motion whatever follows next. So, if our very first, instinctive gut reaction-thought in a given situation, be it during roller-skating, abseiling, or chairing a committee meeting, is: "This is fun!" then we might still experience this rush of adrenaline that signals a state of higher alertness to the body and makes us function better. We experience an increased blood flow to the extremities, our heart beats faster, maybe our palms are sweating slightly. Even the little tightening of the stomach can accompany the anticipation of something pleasant. And we feel this, maybe even take conscious notice of it - but feel alright!

Fun and Fear

This tension while doing something other than "normal" has an element of playfulness and is an integral part of all leisure and pastime activities, of fun. In the case of anticipated fun we notice similar physical symptoms, but we don't shrink from them in horror. It doesn't shake us up. What we do is notice it and embrace it because this is exactly what makes an unusual activity thrilling and exciting! That is exactly what drives people to fun fairs and theme park rides, to extreme sports and horror movies. Many people love this combination of fear and fun. It is an emotional state with its accompanying physical sensations. And we all know that the opposite of this, a clear, rational thinking process, is never, well, hardly ever, accompanied by similar physical sensations. The reason why we seek pleasurable activities is because we like to experience this interplay between body and mind: Feeling fear – experiencing the physical responses - conquering the feeling by rational thoughts such as: "It's not really dangerous" – and riding it out with the determined appraisal that this is fun. It makes us feel alive! Sometimes the risky activity can trigger feelings on the borderline between pleasure and dread, and some people actively enjoy this because it makes them feel in control to play with it and master it.

We love our thrills, after all!

But if our instinctive thought response in a situation, whether it's rock climbing or going on an escalator, is: "I am too high from the safety of the ground. I am in danger. I will fall and get injured. I will fail", then it sets in motion the same whole chain of physical reactions and sensations described above which in turn, in a negative loop, cause further thought processes, feelings and behaviours. The end result in this case is not FUN but FEAR, an unease, a strong negative reaction that can take a powerful hold on our conscious brain and physical self for quite a while. And whether the behaviour reaction is flight, fight or freeze, the set of physiological responses is the same.

What causes the difference in our response is the kind of thought. Our rational brain, the neo-cortex, is equipped not only to undergo logical-rational thinking processes, but also to examine these and, if inappropriate, change or discard them. By defining and redefining the triggering thought, we will in most cases be able to influence undesirable responses of mind, body, and behaviour, like panic and anxiety.

That's the theory so far. And it works in many cases. But in cases when the underlying set of emotional memories, messages, and imprints on the brain are old, entrenched and strong, the "catch-the-thought"-strategy sometimes seems to fight a losing battle.

Sometimes thinking doesn't help

Let's look at Peter. Peter is 45, a successful businessman, who recently experienced very frightening panic attacks seemingly "out of nowhere". They happened frequently, sometimes twice a day: during a business presentation, when he nearly fainted, in a motorway traffic jam on the way back from a conference, during a relaxing weekend away on a sailing boat. Every time the same set of frightening physical sensations: The tightening of the chest, shortness of breath, dizziness, sweating, palpitations. When it happened the first time, Peter was sure he was suffering a heart attack. He was taken to hospital in an ambulance, given the physical all clear very soon after admittance and was then provided with an explanation of what this syndrome was about: A panic attack, very common, very unpleasant. Next time it happens, he was told, try to calm yourself. If you have paper bag at hand, breathe in and out of it in order to neutralise the carbon-dioxide in the blood caused by the hyperventilation, and "ride it out". Peter didn't find this very reassuring. He kept having these crippling attacks more and more often and even though the initial catastrophic thought "I'm going to die of a heart attack" subsided somewhat, he nevertheless felt haunted by these attacks and feared the fear he felt the first time more than anything else.

Panic strikes out of the blue when we least expect it

Someone recommended cognitive-behavioural therapy. Peter so far had scorned all sorts of therapy, thinking it was only for women or self obsessed wimps, not for successful men of the business world. In the end, terrified by his attacks, he made an appointment for an assessment with a counsellor.

After having listened to his story, the therapist explained what I have briefly described above. The fact that his condition had a name, "panic attacks", and the information that many people, men as well as women, suffered from it somewhat reassured Peter. He also took to the model that the therapist drew on a piece of paper for him: The cycle of thought – feeling – physical sensation – behaviour, and how to break it at the point of thought. Now the whole thing sounded more like something that could be cracked in his normal way of dealing with problems: By splitting up a problem into manageable portions and applying logic and rational thinking in order to solve them one by one.

Like with Fred, it worked, but it took a long time. Peter didn't conquer his fear by capturing "hot thoughts", that triggered the attacks, but rather by discovering deep underlying terrifying feelings that had been with him for a long time. In therapy, a memory slowly emerged that Peter had experienced a similar feeling of strong fear apparently out of context when he was much younger. He had been sent to boarding school at a very early age – he was only six – and the day his parents took him there, he was not quite sure what was happening to him. There was a strong sense of uncertainty. Not even when he watched his parent's car leaving down the long drive away from the grey forbidding looking manor house that now would be his "home" for the major part of the year, did he know for sure what was happening. Nobody had really told him. He could barely tolerate the feeling of dread that was sinking down on him like a heavy weight, tightening his stomach, making his little hands sweat. Being in a group with other boys, he didn't dare to show his feelings and he was too young to give it a name anyway: fear of being abandoned, feeling rejected, feeling dangerously alone and trapped.

In the safety of the therapy room he managed to go back into those dreadful feelings. He was able to relive them, name them, and acknowledge them. He also found a connection to very similar issues he was experiencing at this later stage of his life: More and more he had feelings of being all alone, of being unsafe and abandoned. It was as if he had dragged the feelings "up" onto the conscious level where they could be examined and explored. Once they were out, they lost a good part of their scariness.

Encouraged by his therapist, from then on he could look at the panic attacks differently when they happened. He managed to approach them with more rational knowledge and acknowledgement of himself in his mind. He learned how to counter the devastating feelings of "I'm trapped," and "I'm all alone" by other, more realistic thoughts, and the attacks slowly subsided and became manageable. It didn't mean, however, that the dreadful memories were now erased from the back of his mind. It was rather that a connection had been forged into the conscious part of his brain. They were dragged into the awareness of the neo-cortex and therefore made accessible and "tamed". Back in the emotional memory part of the brain, these feelings were uncontrollable and likely to jump out at him at the slightest trigger of vaguely similar situations.

What Peter learned in therapy was not only how to access those fearful memories safely but also to come to some truce with them: Knowing them, acknowledging them and accepting them as part of his unique self.

Know your particular fear, acknowledge it and accept it as part of your unique self

---

Peter's and Fred's stories are examples of how therapy, be it cognitive behavioural, psycho-dynamic or person-centred, can help people who suffer from debilitating panic attacks to gain a more satisfactory life – a life free from very strong and undesirable feelings. Therapy in this sense is not so much about some kind of "healing" but about getting to know yourself better. "Psychotherapy and psychoanalysis are not about what is known and predictable so much as about what needs understanding, what needs accounting for, what the therapist needs to stay open for, what it might be possible to understand and how curiosity can be fruitfully pursued."*

Not Always a Cure

But it doesn't always work, partly for the following reasons.
Even though we assume that fear is one of the oldest, if not the oldest of our emotions, we still don't know exactly what happens in our brain when we feel it. Scientific research so far has not found our emotions important enough to spend much time or money on them. Maybe the reason is that our feelings are considered a slippery fish, not really tangible. Therefore, it was assumed so far that nothing "real" could be at the bottom of feelings, unlike with the other, physiological processes in our body.

---

* Orbach, 1999, p.91

As science slowly works towards a kind of mapping of the brain and further and further explores the electrical and chemical processes between the millions of tiny "seats" of thought, the synapses, we learn more and more about the basics underlying not just thoughts, but also emotions. It all boils down to well-known physical processes – chemical reactions and the transmission of electrical impulses. What we don't know is the actual form and shape of a "feeling", a "memory", a conscious "recognition" or a strong "emotion" like anger.

The Look of Fear
Let's have a look what we do know at this stage:
We know that the amygdala, (Greek for almond) a small almond-sized and -shaped small area in the middle of our brain is most likely to be the "seat" of fear and panic. Among other things this has been suggested by tests on primates, baboons, to be precise, who had their amygdala "lesioned", i.e. artificially damaged. (These tests happened in the Forties, before the debate about the appropriateness of animal testing.) After the operation, the animals showed a remarkable lack of fear.
(Harvey Black, 2001)

Today our main concern...
Today I would have talked about amygdala,
almond-shaped clusters of inter-connected structures
perched above the brain stem –

but today was ominous:
inner and outer weather mingled around the campus
in a tide of cobalt clouds.

THE COMPLETE GUIDE TO GETTING THROUGH IT

Amygdala, little almond,
I would have told them it was you who runs these loops
of low-grade melodrama –

but a gull was crying
above the temple of the Arts Block
as if it had forgotten the sea.

I would have taken them through the limbic system
and the ancestral environments of our feelings,
explained the neural hi-jackings

but feared I might be mad myself,
sing turmoil at them,
sing the syrupy vernacular of the heart

and they'd be waiting
faceless, rising tier on tier like placid saints,
the dispassionate white screen waiting

to be scrawled with the graffiti of fret and angst,
the PA system sense the drowning hollows
of my voice and boom uncertainty.

Today our main concern ... our main concern will be
the cohorts of our intimate enemies,
the toxic thoughts, the case of love…

(Judy Gahagan, 2003)

Scientists are also quite sure that several major nerves run through this amygdala connecting it with some other important brain areas, such as the neo-cortex, the centre of cognition – where our thinking processes take place -, and to the visual cortex, the "seeing bit", where most outside information is received.

It is assumed that during evolution, with the development of the neo-cortex, the "higher brain", the amygdala was being fed more and more external information, making the triggered emotions and emotion-related behaviour increasingly complex. The more input our senses can process on the conscious, the neo cortex level, the more complex our emotions and feelings will be. For today's living with its constant flood of bits of information, this might sometimes lead to a simple "overload" of the brain so that appropriate emotional responses are temporarily suspended or going wrong.

Sometimes we suffer from an overload of information – too much for our brain to process

---

However, so far the human brain has proved to be a very flexible organ with a seemingly unlimited capacity of adapting and changing. We are not born with a fixed brain space but rather with a blueprint for lifelong learning. Whatever we experience, perceive or do, it alters our brain somewhat. Furthermore, we are consciously and unconsciously able to alter our neural pathways. An example of this is any new learning that we endeavour.

Every bit of new learning alters our brain

As described above, if you, for example, would try to learn Spanish and had to start from scratch, without previous experience or exposure, you would start creating a completely new set of neural pathways in your brain by simply memorising the new words and grammatical structures. By sticking to daily routines of learning a few more words and sentences, new paths would get mapped out that would get reinforced and interconnected with other places in your brain as soon as you moved into a Spanish speaking country and applied this knowledge on a day-to-day basis. Under a scanner, your brain would show increased electrical activity in an area that was rather dull and grey before. And so far, the only limit for our brain is the limited time we can apply to new experiences...

There is unlimited space for learning "up there"

Another evidence for the assumption that more complex input results in more complex emotions, could be the tests on rat's brains in the Sixties, similar to those on monkeys described above. Again, their amygdala was interfered with, but the tests did not result in equally striking changes of their fearful behaviour. Remember, the monkeys stopped showing fear altogether.

Rats normally do show signs of fear, but as they have a less developed neo-cortex, they probably display that emotion in connection with a more limited number of triggers to begin with. More developed mammals, however, like primates, process an increasing number of sensory inputs from the outside world – by sight, smell, hearing, touch and taste - that can potentially trigger fear. So, the more highly developed the brain is, the more it processes outside stimuli, the higher the potential for experiencing fear, as the number of fear-triggers that get processed by the brain increases.

Our brains are confronted by billions of bits of information on a daily basis that realistically cannot all be processed by the brain. Therefore, we have a kind of in-built "threshold", a barrier that excludes automatically the kind of input from the outside that is deemed unnecessary. We know how that works, because when we are engrossed in some activity, we automatically exclude most of what is going on around us (see Part II, p. 94). In a state of curiosity, though, e.g. when arriving in a foreign place, our senses are heightened to a maximum intake of external stimuli. This "taking in everything" might contribute to the commonly experienced feeling on holiday that the first few days always seem incredibly long, whereas towards the end of the trip days just rush by. In this first phase everything is new to us, and we are confronted with a much larger number of stimuli, which, once processed, won't ask for the same brain space afterwards anymore. On days at home, however, when nothing new seems to happen, time appears to stretch, and the brain tends to slow down, too. It is as if the brain automatically adjusts its input threshold according to what it feels able to process at any given moment.

There is a theory stating that some people who are more easily triggered to fear and other feelings generally have a lower "threshold", so all the time more information gets to the processors in the brain than they can handle. This might lead to breakdowns in the nerve circuits which in turn can cause panicking. If that should be the case, it would be a problematic condition for any countering strategy such as "tracing hot thoughts". Maybe calming approaches such as a different lifestyle, meditation, yoga etcetera would be more effective in order to deal with incoming stimuli more effectively. This is only one theory about the susceptibility to panic attacks and while there is no proof or refutation, we can only try out whether relief can be found by such calming approaches.

A First Map of the Brain

The tests of animal's amygdala and the results described above go back a number of years. Only in the seventies, with the development of magnetic resonance imaging (MRI Scanners) further and more detailed research was possible. Scientists could now really start to map out the brain by checking what was happening electrically in the grey matter following certain triggers. They could now observe how visual input, something we see, caused electrical activity in the visual cortex, the one fed by the optical nerve. This clarified among other things which parts of the brain were specialised for which activity and on which pathways external and internal information was processed.

One of the tests carried out consisted of showing pictures of frightening situations to a number of people. The MRI scans showed a steep increase of electrical activity in the amygdala - the little almond-shaped organ in the middle of the brain – that rapidly subsided again. For the first time, a human being could observe what fear looked like in the brain of another person: A short outburst of electrical activity – short and sharp as a shock, a sudden startle like when we are woken in the middle of the night by a loud noise. In a flash all our senses are on red alert, peak in a fraction of a second and then gradually subside after we have determined that the bang was caused by nothing more dangerous than the alarm clock falling off the bedside table, knocked over by our sleeping self whilst turning round.

Fear and Panic
So, since the Seventies of last century not only do we know what fear feels like – and we've known that since our fore-creatures lived in the water – we also know what fear looks like on an MRI Scanner.

But scientists have discovered another fact about fear and that discovery can change the way we have so far tried to tackle its debilitating cousin, unreal fear and panic attacks.

Let's go back to Fran first, the woman confronted by her past in the shape of an ex-boyfriend who had gone "mad" and had threatened her life.

Fran unexpectedly spotted Tom in her home town. She experienced acute, sharp fear – triggered by her memory of how he had threatened her with a knife, and of her narrow escape.

After that initial shock, Fran calmed down somewhat, and so did her fast heart-rate. The sweating and the tightness in her stomach all subsided – all those familiar feelings associated not only with that specific fear from a few years back, but with older, more generalised feelings of dread and survival. What followed next, corresponds to the pattern we have described above: A thought emerged, a thought that said: "I am in danger because Tom will threaten me and he might kill me." And then, with this clear-cut, rational thought at hand, Fran did not break out into more panic, but could take this thought and continue along the more rational lines of: "He might have changed. I am not in immediate danger. What I will do now is…" And then her logical, analytical mind took over to make appropriate plans of how to avoid a chance encounter and how to find out more about Tom's whereabouts through mutual former friends and his family. Reassured by this taking control of her thoughts, and feeling calmer, Fran could move on, feeling more alert to a possible danger than before, but able to function and deal with it in a rational way.

Somehow, this "normal" way of dealing with a fearful situation shows us to what an extent rational, cognitive thinking is part of the process. Immediately after the first emotive shock, thoughts muscle in and, like in a committee meeting, debate the case against the panic and win.

Negative emotions flood us much more strongly than positive ones

The trouble is that emotions, like fear, easily dispel other events out of the foreground of the mind – but never the other way around. Sadness or depression for example cannot be dispelled by positive thoughts alone. They just happen to us and are very powerful in flooding the consciousness and disabling it. Unfortunately not the same is true for pleasant feelings like happiness and contentment. Fran's fear was "real". What about Gina and her being flooded by "unreal" panic?

Unreal thoughts

We have heard that Gina experienced attacks of sharp fear, like panic, very unexpectedly in situations that bore no signs of imminent or even potential danger. Her last panic attack occurred after she had started seeing a counsellor and unravelled some of the entangled processes of thought, feeling, sensations and behaviour. She was driving a couple of colleagues to a training seminar about 30 miles away to an educational centre. The four women were in a good mood – they were looking forward to a couple of days learning new skills in a pleasant environment, with good food – on full pay. A welcome break from the often stressful work. After half an hour, Gina, who was driving, suddenly and without an apparent trigger, felt the first rush of panic, like an aura. She knew what was going to happen: She thought she was falling to pieces and start crying uncontrollably – and she panicked. What if her colleagues witnessed her being the helpless victim of a crippling fear, crying, panting, sweating, being completely out of control? This fear of the fear increased the feeling of dread sinking down on her. She gave in – or rather caved in – pulled over on to the hard shoulder and broke down crying. Her colleagues, nonplussed, tried in vain and for a long time to comfort her, until she finally calmed down, drained and exhausted.

Floods of Tears and Emotions

What we notice here is, that at no point between the onset and the slow recovery from the attack did a rational thought come in: At the first signs, Gina panics and panic prevents rational thinking.

Giving in to the fear is a simple giving up, not connected to any rational thought such as that it would be dangerous to carry on driving. Only sheer exhaustion finally brings the episode to an end, not, like with Fran, a calmer and calming approach to the problem at hand.

Panic takes its own course

Another difference is that there is no apparent problem at hand that could be solved. The whole process happens on an emotional level – that's how we express ourselves before the brain comes in. If the building blocks of the emotion of fear are neural systems that regulate physical and behavioural responses to activate us for survival, then just "feeling fearful" is not enough – for survival it needs the physical and behavioural "gut-response". A panic attack seems to be de-coupled from that survival response.

Panic attacks are de-coupled from our survival response

The third difference is the afore mentioned absence of rational thoughts. According to the cognitive behavioural model, the thought is the point of entry to the cycle of fear, enabling us to alter the chain of events. But what if in a fully blown panic attack there is no such a thing? When the only thoughts are: "This is a panic attack and I'm terrified"? What if there is no apparent problem at hand? What, if cognitive perception and processing are temporarily out of order - overridden or bypassed by powerful

emotions that only die down by wearing themselves out?
Somehow a panic attack seems to be a scenario where the connections between the feeling of fear and the rational, physical and behavioural responses are missing or out of kilter which makes it very difficult to be approached on those levels. This means that we can only tackle the panic on the level on which it is happening – the emotional one. Gina instinctively took that road of "riding it out". She had no choice other than taking the fear on fully frontally and letting it exhaust itself. The amygdala, as has been shown, has a limited capacity and loses its regulatory impact on physical reactions after a while. That means that the hormonal output it triggers decreases automatically after a while and with it the frightening physical sensations.

The amygdala exhausts itself after a while – every feeling of fear or panic comes to its natural end

---

After a prolonged output of adrenaline, the amygdala falters. The emotional shortcuts are weakened and the focussing on conscious thoughts to counteract the fear can be strengthened.

So only after allowing the fear to flood us and in a state of mental and physical exhaustion can rational thoughts slowly slip in to restore balance. For Gina this meant not only to acknowledge how powerful her old fears were, but also to be open about it towards her colleagues and friends. After this strong attack, which she fully rode out, her panicky feelings became less frequent and less overwhelming.

Lethal Panic

Our third fear scenario gives us further clues as to how to tackle fear and its crippling cousin, panic:

When the fight broke out in the Chicago disco, the stewards sprayed tear gas into the crowd. It is assumed that the majority, or just some of the young people around the affray interpreted the situation fatally wrong, triggered by the chemical smell. Having being subjected to numerous press articles and radio programmes about possible terrorist attacks in the weeks previously, they were conditioned to a state of alert which was way beyond the real situation. Terrible fear set in where normal wariness and common sense would have been sufficient.

We can only assume what would have happened without that conditioning. Maybe there would not have been the high level of alertness to "chemical" smells spelling immediate danger to a large number of victims. Without that conditioning there might have been a bigger chance that most people around the incident would have either recognized the smell as teargas and would have come to the right conclusion that there was a safety incident, not a security one. Without the actual, focussed fear conditioning, they would have interpreted the danger signals more appropriately.

There would still have been a strong urge in the young people to escape from an unpleasant situation, but the situation would not have been wrongly interpreted as potentially lethal. The chance of a stampede happening and killing nearly thirty young people would have been much smaller.

What happened in the brains of the disco goers – and again, we can only assume – was a dangerously wrong rational interpretation of danger signals. There was a rational thought – "This is a terrorist attack!" – and exactly that triggered the out of control fear and panic. But the thought was un-real, not based on a real danger, and with catastrophic results. At no point during this crisis was there a chance to examine this thought based on false information, so no rationality could come in, like with Fran.

We can consider this a "conditioned" fear – the same kind as all our instinctive fears (such as fear of heights, of snakes, of fire and water) – which, through experience and observation, have been programmed into our brain. We have described above how the brain – the emotional as well as the rational one – is an incredibly flexible organ. This means that complete new sets of trigger-response mechanisms can be conditioned and hardwired into it. That way, a faintly chemical smell, an abandoned bag in a crowded railway station, a person following in the same direction behind us when we are walking home late at night can be potential sources of great danger – and trigger a strong fear in us.

In his recent film "Bowling for Columbine", the director Michael Moore described in frightening detail how a general condition of underlying fear of attackers seems to have been conditioned into the American psyche in general since the early days of the first settlers. The then real fear of native attackers or wild creatures, of perishing in the wilderness, was over time translated into the defence attitude of wearing a gun. The frighteningly high figures of gun crime in the US may be a direct result from this programmed fear of an attack. In a state of relative paranoia and having a gun ready at all times, it is very easy to pull the trigger. Comparative figures from other societies, markedly from Canada where the gun laws and the frequency of gun carrying are the same but where the figures for gun crime are negligible, hardly leave any other conclusion than that unreal fear is at the bottom of this sad statistics in the US. It's the same unreal fear that worsened the survival chances of the young people in the Chicago disco.

Brains learn fast and de-learn slowly

It appears from research so far, that the flexibility of the brain to create new processes is one of its main features. The process the other way around, however, is not so easy. It seems that "de-learning" is by far slower and maybe ultimately impossible. What has been stored "up there" once, is there to stay, be it in a conscious or subconscious way or deeply buried in our unconscious memory.

Sigmund Freud, the father of psychoanalysis, had already recognized this clearly. In the early paper "Beyond the Pleasure Principle" he hypothesises that when experiencing trauma, the human mind is flooded with stimuli that it is unable to process in the normal way – hence the resulting feelings of, at best, being disturbed, at worst, experiencing psychosis or a complete mental breakdown while shutting away the memory of the traumatic event. But it is there. Other events later on can stir up these earlier ones and connect them to the same feeling of devastation, of complete helplessness, of the feeling that the mind can't cope, that have been kept in "a sealed pocket of vulnerability whose existence forms a constant threat to stability. ... and earlier anxieties... invade the ego. The experience of an an external traumatic event will open up such pockets of disturbance, and through the process of binding, keep them open, giving their contents fresh life and imbuing the present with the significance of the past." (Garland, 1998, p 19) In other words, the brain hardly forgets anything.

Rationing Doesn't Come In

Looking at our three fear stories again, we notice now that there are different processes at work – a rational one in the first case, whereas in the two others rational thinking is remarkably absent.

But what is happening? We find some answers in more recent research. For example, it was discovered that the amygdala is subdivided into various different parts that deal with various forms of fear. This little organ can be partitioned off into seats of anxiousness, of fear and of panic, and it looks like these also involve different processes and responses.

Different kinds of fears – different brain processes

Different Kinds of Fear

Let's look at the different kinds of fear. First, Anxiety. This could be described as a more low-key, permanent stage of fear, with a constantly raised level of amygdala activity and chemical exchange. The anxious body is on a permanent "orange" light rather than "green". Acute fear would be dealt with in a quick response allowing a rapid chain of responses, maybe thought processes and a subsequent dying down of amygdala activity. With anxiety, these levels and the accompanying output of stress hormones are constantly higher. This could be described either as a malfunction or as an evolutionary adaptation to an increased number of outside stimuli or stressors to be processed by an increasingly complex brain.

Fear originally was the response to acute, short term stressors, like an attack by a wolf or a sabre tooth tiger, causing the following chain of events:

Attack – attacker perceived – fear – mobilisation of physical responses – physical response – calming down (or death).

Compared to this mechanism, anxiety these days is caused by more low key, long-term stressors like constant noise, overcrowding, real and presumed dangers of road traffic, of crime, of terrorist attacks etcetera. There is a theory saying that this modern day situation, with a constant barrage of potential "attacks" as listed above, trigger the over-functioning of the amygdala's old fear response into overdrive, into a malfunction. We then live not only "on our nerves" but with a higher level of adrenaline output than appropriate and normal, causing a kind of constant physical and emotional reaction. Today's hectic life provides the brain with many more triggers for being alerted, alarmed, startled, made wary – maybe too many for some people to cope with.

Freud distinguished between automatic anxiety, which would be our in-built survival response to an actual danger, and signal anxiety, an anxious state when a danger is threatening. This signal anxiety is only a warning. Garland (1998) holds that when a person has experienced a traumatic situation at some stage in his or her life, she/he cannot afford to believe in signal anxiety anymore: "In any situation resembling the life-threatening trauma the individual behaves as if it were flooded with automatic anxiety...Certain smells, sounds, sights, situations, even words connected with the traumatic event all produce states of immense anxiety...There is no capacity and no place for belief in 'signals' or 'warning'. This is it."

What this means for the person flooded by "unreasonable" fear is described in the cases of Peter and Jim. They responded to "signals", somehow similar or related triggers, as if to a real danger. With the help of a counsellor/therapist they needed to revisit their past and trace where their feelings connected to a traumatic event in order to again be able to distinguish "real" danger and mere warnings.

The Stress of It

Stress, of course, with its increased output of adrenaline is one of the physical companions of acute fear. While initially stress enhances the brain functions and our conditioned responses – making us feel alert and alive -, too much of it has long-term effects on us. In a state of permanent high alert, or constant stress, all learning and therefore the formation of memories is impaired.

Under stress, all learning is impaired

Stress has an impact on the higher brain functions and this robs us of conscious choices. In that condition we can only react, not consciously choose a way out of a situation. Severe stress is also known to damage the receptors on our unconscious brain which in extreme cases can lead to total memory loss.

Continuous stress in some parts of our life can, through the continuous over-stimulation of the amygdala, trigger anxiety disorders, when dealing with fearful thoughts take over the day-to-day functioning. Again, this points to an "overload" of external triggers and input.

What this means is obvious but not always easy to balance out. We have to explore the areas of our life that cause continuous stress to find out what can be changed for the better. This might apply to apparently completely unrelated areas of our lives – like with Gina - but with the effect that the underlying anxiety with its tendency to erupt into panic seemingly out of the blue will subside. Sometimes the process of finding out where and when we are stressed and under more demand than we can cope with takes a good while and needs facilitating by a counsellor or therapist. After all, we have devised our own clever strategies for coping and they sometimes have worked for a long time. But it takes the literal straw that breaks the camel's back to undo them altogether.

For Diane it had worked for twenty years: She lived in a marriage without love, and she had managed (covered up, really) the feelings of great emptiness and longing for being loved. Her first strategy was having one baby after the other – five all in all. Every time she was pregnant, she had convinced herself that life would now be better, that her husband really, deep down, loved her. The love she felt for the new baby also sustained her for a while. Her husband, however, stayed the same throughout: Detached, cold, not appreciative and more and more under pressure to provide for the growing family.

When the children were all at school at last, Diane started "collecting jobs" She took on whatever was on offer. At the point when she finally admitted to being completely stressed out she had five part-time jobs and worked as a volunteer in two more functions apart from looking after her large family.

She wasn't aware that she had been on red alert from all the pressure for a long time. Over the years all those demands had completely worn her out and lowered her defences so that she broke down with high anxiety and nervous exhaustion.

Looking at *her* areas of possible stress was easy. What was more difficult was to scale down her responsibilities and face the real dissatisfaction underneath – the lack of love that had sent her into this life in overdrive.

Again, the model of focussing on conscious thoughts to conquer fear and panic, is not sufficient. It needs some more present and future focussed changes in the whole of our life to come to grips with "unreasonable" fear and whatever might lie behind it.

Panic, the high alert emergency mode, could also be considered to be a malfunction, because other than with "normal" fear it doesn't allow thought processes to interfere in order to neutralise the fear stimulus. Panic is such an exaggerated and debilitating state of fear that it feeds on itself. With rational thought processes being side-tracked, in a state of panic we can't and don't interpret the apparent danger properly and jump to wrong conclusions – like Gina and the young people in the disco.

Panic is a state that fuels on itself

Here we come across a first indication that those frenzies of fear apparently out of the blue and what we commonly know as "panic attacks" can be traced back to an amygdala in overdrive. We will come back to this later. We have already mentioned the different pathways of how external information is processed. With panic, the information goes straight to the amygdala and causes the automatic fear response of the body without involving the cortex and a rational evaluation at all. With panic attacks, the thinking doesn't kick in afterwards either, as it would normally do to evaluate the trigger properly in good time. Thus we stay in "panic mode", as if the neural path back to thinking processes is somehow blocked.

Our survival depended on fast automatic responses

With "normal" fear, the feedback loop back to the cortex where input gets rationally processed, occurs later and much slower than the "fast track" from first perception to the fear-centre, the amygdala, and from there to the various parts of the body. This reaction is automatic and more or less imminent. It can be explained by going back to the early days of our history: When faced by an imminent physical danger, by a lion or a tiger, the most important thing was to get physically ready to face that threat. So the fastest reactions we are programmed to perform are the instinctive ones: freeze, fight or flight. If the danger should turn out not to be very real or just perceived – a cracking of twigs was caused by a hedgehog rather than by a wolf – at least it couldn't do much harm to have been alerted to the worst case scenario. This serves also as evidence that panic attacks never do any harm, and one doesn't die of them. After all, our bodies are programmed quite cleverly to react this way rather more often than not.

The much slower conscious appraisal mode, when we rationally weigh up different options and only then make the decision to go on red alert or not, would not have been the best survival method. Therefore, we initially always respond with the lightning fast automatic processing of triggers caused by the amygdala to put the physical reactions into gear. The way back though, the slow-down, is, as we have mentioned, not so fast and not really pre-programmed, as it is not relevant for survival.

Knowing that, we can see now how it comes that emotions/feelings seem somehow to flood us and trigger distinctive physical reactions, whereas rational thoughts, the actual process of thinking, "feel" totally different.

Thoughts are rarely accompanied by a physical sensation

They hardly ever "flood" us - whereas there are no body-less emotions! We cannot even imagine that we experience fear, or hatred, or jealousy without the specific physical signs. This is due to the hardwiring of our brain and to the fact that the neural pathways are so fast that we are able to respond very quickly to certain triggers. Afterwards and much more slowly we use different neural paths to appraise the situation with the "thinking bit" of the brain, the neo-cortex. And the thinking doesn't need the physical signs to alert us and get us in fighting or fleeing mode

There is also some recent research of how different parts of the amygdala show a different cell structure, indicating that the "seats" for fear and panic are different. This would confirm that their expression in terms of behaviour would be different as well. Fear and Panic, however, are closely related negative emotions. Both have in common the above described pathway, the super highway "straight into the heart" of the amygdala, rather than via the B-road of conscious thinking and evaluation. Maybe the path of panic is a hyperlink to physical responses and behaviour, bypassing even the instinctive fear response of fight or flight and resulting in a rather complete disintegration of reactions.

What that means for the person suffering from panic attacks is, that in the face of the fast instinctive reaction of the brain and the body and the delayed response of the "thinking" brain, there is little chance to counter the crippling attacks by conscious thoughts, as advocated by cognitive therapy. We will have to accept that first and foremost we are experiencing on the feeling level, and so it follows that we have to start from there. We need different strategies for coming to grips with panic.

For managing panic we need different strategies

There are other possible explanations for panic attacks. Clark (1988) sees them as "as a maladaptive and faulty interpretation of body signals". But how does this "maladaptive interpretation" happen, and what does it look like? Is it of a chemical or an electrical nature? What causes it to become faulty? Does it happen *after* the "body signals"?

Genetic Disposition or Neural Development?
Some scientists assume a genetic disposition nurtured by a tendency to catastrophic thinking. How would that happen? And why? What consequences would this have in regard to a therapeutic process towards making feelings of exaggerated fear manageable or even tolerable?

Even if the tendency to feel fear would be based in our genes, the effect would be the same. We would still have to deal with unreasonable and exaggerated fear. The conclusions would be the same – but maybe the de-learning of fear responses would be even more difficult.

Holt (1998), based on more detailed research, questions the statement that "the amygdala is the seat of fear" by stating that since it has been found to have up to 22 subgroups, only 2 so far have been reliably identified with a flight response. The other responses, defence and aggression, apparently are processed or triggered in other parts. There are numerous other parts of the almond-shaped organ not as yet defined or explained. Holt's conclusion is that dealing with fear is not the main task of the amygdala. This would mean that other parts of the brain are involved in the process of trigger – fear response – calming down and, given the complexity of the brain and how little we have explored of it so far, this could trigger further research of our emotions in general.

These are all recent observations. At the bottom of them, however, is a neuro-biological fact. The underlying structure for different "centres", different trigger-responses, different behaviour, different forms of expression, **is a network of neural pathways through our brain that constantly creates different <u>circuits</u> for different functions.** This "circuitry" can throw a completely new light on the ways we deal with fear, anxiety and panic attacks. We don't deal anymore with a potentially fixed universe of our brain where every aspect of our mind has its seat or process, but with a constant flux and changing and changeable patterns of how we respond to the world outside.

It is as if the universe of our mind mirrors the world out there in its complexity and infinite potential for changes

---

This means that we can by experience, observation and learning create or strengthen neural pathways that serve us better

Different Kinds of Processes

We have seen that there are at least two different ways of processing "sensory input" – what we perceive through our senses. We "… know of the amygdala that it has a dual sensory input system. Both inputs run from the eyes, ears, and other sensory organs to the thalamus. At that point, the inputs diverge. One pathway leads directly to the amygdala while the other first runs through the cortex. Each input causes a distinct and specialised behaviour. The amygdala is specialised to respond to stimuli and to triggering a physiological response, a process that would be described as the "emotion" of fear. After this, the stimuli of the activation of the amygdala are transmitted to the cortex. This is a distinct difference from a conscious feeling of fear. Feelings are thought to arise from the second, slower pathway that travels from the sensory input first to the higher cortex and then to the amygdala. In the cortex the frightening stimulus is analysed in detail, using information from many parts of the brain, and a message is sent back to the amygdala." (Holt)

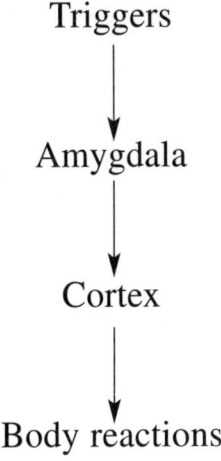

In other words, outside events that can trigger a fear response, are fed into our brain on different ways. After being perceived the normal way through our eyes, ears, nose and touch, the information is passed on in two different ways – on the "super highway" straight to the amygdala to trigger the physical responses, and on the "B-road" back to the cortex where the much slower rational thinking and evaluating takes place.

This dual mechanism seems a bit superfluous at first sight, but turns out to be invaluable. The very first, direct signals to the amygdala seem to have the function that the proper physical reactions to a perceived danger are in place. To be quick is first priority. Then, and only then, the stimulus gets processed in the cortex in a cognitive analytical way. The signs get analysed and evaluated, with the result that the fear response is either called back, and the amygdala activity dies down, or they get confirmed as dangerous and then more complex information about how to deal with the frightening situation is generated.

This impressive dual system has a drawback, though, which is probably another culprit responsible for the "fear going haywire". The wiring, the neural pathways from the cortex to the amygdala are less well developed than vice versa, than the pathways from the amygdala to the cortex, meaning that the fear responses from the amygdala are considerably stronger than the rational-analytical information from the cortex.

Our brain is hardwired in an old-fashioned non-thinking way

This means that the "irrational" fear can overpower our rational thinking any time and override a possibly more balanced reaction to a perceived danger. So, gut reactions neurologically are much faster and stronger than conscious considerations. And again this helps explain that the conscious, cognitive approach to counter exaggerated fear is sometimes not the most effective.

With these facts in mind, let's look at Fran, Gina and the young people in the disco again.

With Fran, we have seen that she was able to muscle in with rational thoughts, after the first initial shock of fear at the sudden and unexpected confrontation with a memory of danger had set in. This enabled her to think more clearly and make plans of how to cope with the risky situation. We can also assume that her considerations on which she based her plans and decisions, were appropriate to the situation. That means, she didn't immediately call the police to have her old lover arrested, nor did she walk straight towards him to hug him as an old friend to say hello. Her response pattern was:

shock – stop – think – plan – act.

With Gina, we see a different picture. Gina was gripped by an irrational fear. In terms of neural pathways, there seemed to have been a direct feed from some external trigger, unrecognized by her, to the amygdala. Not being consciously aware of the trigger, it could not rationally be evaluated. By bypassing the cortex and its function to add rational elements, her fear stayed unchecked and could blossom into a crippling attack.

No cortex involvement - no thought processes - no breaking of the cycle - no cognitive behavioural mastering of the fear process

Her only option was to break down, to give in to it and to let her fear die down with exhaustion.

We have stated before that the amygdala, after prolonged output of adrenaline, falters and loses its regulatory function. Only then the emotional shortcut-path to it is weakened and the focussing on conscious thoughts to counteract the fear can be strengthened. It means that only when the fear has been "ridden out" fully, thoughts can be "slipped in" to balance the emotion out.

"Unknown" Causes
There is an interesting concept that might find a place here:

"infantile amnesia" – the fact that some people have a strong phobic fear of, say, snakes, without a conscious memory of a previous dangerous encounter with such an animal. The reason, however, could be that the circuits that deal with memories in humans mature at a later stage than the neural pathways that deal with fear responses. So, fear experienced as a young baby, before the brain is capable of storing and retrieving conscious memories, inevitably leads to unconscious memories that cannot be accessed later in life. However, they are nevertheless there as we are hardwired to our fear responses for our survival.

I know a young woman with an intense fear of loud sudden banging noises. This is now, after intense behavioural therapy and hypnotherapy, manageable for her, but the fear seems to be "in her bones". Maybe it dates back to a very early experience, at the age of three months, when her parents took her to the top of a church tower to celebrate the New Year. At midnight, the bells began to ring - very close by. The incredibly loud booming penetrated the tower and everybody on it and made them vibrate from the sound-waves. The baby started to howl, the parents took her down and away from the sound as quickly as possible, but this experience may have planted a fear memory into her limbic system that cannot be eradicated. It's in her bones. She cannot consciously remember it, as her neural system was not ready for storing conscious memories. "The strange midnight terror that permeates the bones while your mind, alert and rational, insists that all is normal, there is nothing to be frightened of. But that bone-fear ... is deaf to reason..." (Diski 1987, p. 128)

Research has shown that memories, when formed accompanied by emotions, i.e. by an output of adrenaline, are much stronger and vivid. For example, a whole generation of middle aged people knows where they were on the day President Kennedy was shot more than forty years ago! The shock of the tragic news triggered an adrenaline rush and planted a distinctive memory of the event in their brains.

Memories of experiences under stress are either very strong or blank

These so-called "flashbulb" memories are very durable. In terms of unpleasant early memories, like the one with the church bells, it means that they will always be there, but through behavioural therapy, a conscious, de-sensitizing and de-learning approach, they can be made tolerable and manageable.

So, a reasonable portion of stress can actually enhance a situation and the accompanying memory and make it more vivid and lasting. But what about severe and prolonged stress? We know now that after a long period of exaggerated demands on us, at work or in our private life, our mental ability starts flagging. Perception is hampered, learning is impeded and the formation of explicit memories impaired. Severe stress can actually lead to a shrivelling up of receptors in the hippocampus which leads to a complete memory loss. One syndrome of post traumatic stress disorder is the disproportion of very sharp flashback memories surrounded by a total blank – no memories at all, just a blur.

In this state people are quite susceptible to depression which again has a negative effect on learning and conscious memory forming. It is a vicious cycle, when the brain still perceives and processes information but cannot store them other than unconsciously – from where they can only be retrieved with difficulty but still can have a profound impact on our feeling states and responses. In that way, stress can foster all sorts of anxiety disorders. Recent research has shown that prolonged stress actually alters the structure of some brain parts (the neo-cortex and the hippocampus) which can lead to a shutdown, which in turn has an impact on the amygdala. This breakdown of the normal "brakes" can cause the "revival" of long suppressed or forgotten negative memories, a re-emergence of a fear that we don't really remember.

There is a general consensus that the limbic system (the "old" or stem brain consisting of hippocampus, hypothalamus and amygdala) as the processor of emotions is also involved in generating panic attacks – as if some ancient fears are vaguely remembered and, completely out of context, raise their ugly head from time to time to haunt us. All in all, it is a very complex system – the processing of what we perceive with our senses, and we are only at the beginning of exploring the different ways of dealing with input, processing it, discarding some, and remembering and retrieving other bits of information.

Where Are We Now?
So, where are we at this point? We know now roughly what is happening in our brain, when we feel all sorts of different fears. We know our responses. We have learned that fear memories are practically indelible, they sit in our bones. We have also learned that cognitive therapy in many cases is quite powerless to "train away" anxiety:

"In the future, scientists believe imaging techniques may help determine the course of treatment for disorders involving a malfunction in fear processing. For example, a person with an extreme fear of germs, ... often goes through months of behavioural therapy. The idea is to train the person to learn to overcome their fear. But what if imaging tests show that the amygdala is continuously active and does not diminish its activity over time as it would normally would do... A lifetime of therapy designed to alter behaviour would not be able to stifle the fear response." (Brain Briefings)

This doesn't sound like good news as it somehow undoes what we have been believing and hoping for the last fifty years or so, that fear and anxiety, phobias and general dread could be dealt with either by medication or carefully planned therapy. What are we left with, then?

It's not all bad news, though. All it needs is a slight shift in our view of things. Knowing what we know now about the neural processes in our brain, we can come to a more matter of fact view of things. Fear has been with us and will be with us as humans as "an important part of human existence... fundamental to what is special about humans, but also as a clue to our frailty." (LeDoux, 232).

LeDoux quotes O.H.Mowrer, a behaviourist, to underpin this view: "...that the fact that the forward-looking, anxiety-arousing propensity of the human mind is more highly developed than it is in lower animals probably accounts for many of man's unique accomplishments." (LeDoux, 233)

In other words, **fear is with us and it has a great potential as a drive forward**. We have to learn to live with it, appreciate it as a positive force and make use of it.

"Nature, to be commanded, has to be obeyed" (Francis Bacon)

Part II

"When I Look up at the Stars, I Feel Giddy" –

Alone with Yourself

Part II

"When I Look up at the Stars, I Feel Giddy" –

Alone with Yourself

"When I look up at the stars, it always makes me feel giddy."
These words by my friend Iris bring one thing to a point: It's about where and who we are - tiny pinpricks in a huge universe. It is not only too immense for us to grasp, but also infinite. Many people feel a kind of dread when their thoughts go this way: We know our immediate surroundings – the family, the street, the village, town or city. Maybe we have travelled a bit and got to know some other parts of our planet.

But even if we are acquainted with every square centimetre of the earth, we only just, just know one single planet in our solar system, which again is only a tiny speck in the galaxy, which is only one of countless other systems. Some of those have been spotted by powerful telescopes, but we can assume that there is an infinite number of other systems "out there". Infinite. Getting giddy yet?

Pinpricks on our Planet
Some people are filled with dread by this thought of being infinitely small in an infinitely large, and, according to latest research, constantly expanding environment. It makes them feel utterly unimportant and small, like a single, completely irrelevant and inconsequential flicker of life in total darkness. On for a short time, then extinguished and never to be seen again. Thoughts like that often lead to the question: "What's the point anyway?" And that not only cause giddiness, but also a deep fear.

As this is the condition for all human beings, they have from the very beginnings of their organised life attempted to anchor themselves, to give their life a meaning, a sense, a point in order to quell this fear of the great void.

The Way we Are
One way of being grounded in a more secure way to prevent this feeling of free floating in the big empty space, is to develop a sense of belonging or attachment. We find it by creating systems around us that become familiar – the mere adverb indicating our first and foremost system: the family. Within a framework of known and reliable points of reference, of relatives, friends and acquaintances, we can relax a little, feel secure and can keep the thoughts of what is "out there" at bay.

Mother-child relationships were the first stable units of humankind's budding societal attempts. This was a sure thing: Mothers grow babies in their bellies and give birth to them. They belong together. Before people figured out that it takes a man *and* a woman to make a child, mother and infant were considered as one flesh, as a strong unit, knitted together by the instinctive bond of motherly care.

Attachment

To this day, this first and primary unit between mother and child is vital for the development of a child's emotional state in later life. The way we attach at the beginning of our life has a strong impact on how attached or grounded we feel to other people and aspects of our life.

If the attachment between caregiver and baby is reliable and consistent, the later adult will have developed a strong sense of self-value, confidence and security in the way they deal with the world. There is not much room for unreasonable or exaggerated fear based on doubts and insecurity. The world view is more like: "I know that I can reasonably rely on most things, but not on others, and the latter won't shake me unduly. I can be forward looking and brave and take some risks without the fear of being annihilated."

If the attachment between caregiver and baby is less than secure, if it is not consistent and not always reliable, then the child learns the lesson of: "Sometimes my needs are met, but sometimes not, and that makes me feel quite bad." Any ambivalence like that easily causes anxiety and a fear of loss and separation regardless of the circumstances. An underlying message could be: "I am not worth being looked after in a loving, stable way. I'm not sure whether or not people might reject or abandon me."

If the attachment in the first unit of mother/caregiver and child is not reliable and loving at all, the only message the baby receives is: "My needs don't get met. Better not to expect anything from other people. I have to try and do it all for myself by myself", with the result of emotional self-reliant, independent people who in turn avoid reaching out to others and find it difficult to enter into closer relationships.

The first attachment to our primary caregiver not only sets the way for how we develop towards adulthood, but also has a strong impact on how we see ourselves in the world and how grounded we feel: Either small and insignificant or unique and precious.

The last two of the three types of attachment – anxious and avoidant – probably have a strong impact on the quality of our life. With different outlooks – positive or negative – we live different lives. But once established that way, things don't have to stay like that for good. As we have stated before – and we cannot repeat it often enough – our brain, with its rational and emotional contents, is practically limitless in its capacity to change. Healing, remedial relationships can subtly and slowly alter the attachment way of anxious or avoidant people and nurture a more positive, confident outlook to the world.

Friends and Family

In the development of our human species, the next extension of the mother-baby unit towards a group which could give us a sense of meaning and anchoring was the extended family with women at its centre – matri-centric clans and tribes. Here, not only did the resources get pooled, but there were more people to give each other feedback, encouragement, comfort and nurturing, security and confidence.

When we try and imagine what life was like for stone-age men and women, from about 600.000 BC onwards, we have to picture them huddled together in a place that they knew very well – a cave maybe, by a river, in or near some woodland for hunting and gathering.

No Place like Home

Places further afield were less familiar. Only occasionally, some clan member would venture out, maybe when food was becoming scarce, or for sheer curiosity – which is a strong and utterly human emotion. These quests were accompanied by a good deal of fear, much more than they felt in the vicinity of the place were they lived, cooked, slept and played. Out there was danger. And already we can assume a kind of thrill-feeling, when fear and curiosity teamed up to give a sense of adventure, of risk-taking - a feeling well known to us who pursue extreme sports or not so extreme activities that take us out of the ordinary. Thrill seeking is another way of taming basic fears and has probably been with us as a species for a very long time.

Scary stars

And sometimes at night, with a clear sky, our forefathers and – mothers would have sat by a fire or in the dark and looked up at the night sky with its miraculous phenomena: The moon with its constant waxing and waning, the countless stars which seem to flicker and beckon and indicate other beings out there, the occasional eclipse, when the comparatively familiar face of the moon suddenly was covered by a baleful dark disk obliterating it for a short time. Not knowing about these happenings and their mechanics will only have deepened the fear of the unknown that our ancestors probably felt, a dread of what they did not know. And like Iris in the twenty-first century, they may have avoided looking up and seeing these inexplicable things that might spell great danger, so they would not feel giddy with dread. Turning to the family or clan around them, restricting their eyes to the circle of firelight, would have created comfort and distracted them from thinking of the cold darkness out there.

We are on the same planet as our ancestors, with the same constellations in the sky as then (give and take some changes). It's not surprising that even with all the accumulated knowledge about the universe, with all the astrophysical data available, with telescopes that penetrate ever deeper into the stellar space, we still feel the same dread when we come to consider ourselves and our place in this space. Questions such as "What is it all about?" "What lies beyond?" "What is my role in this?" come just as easily to us as they did to our foremothers and -fathers.

Solace and Comfort
So by and by, as a species, we have found solace and comfort in the people close to us, our family and other friends nearby. To this day, being attached, being grounded and anchored that way gives us a great feeling of being content and safe. That is one of the reasons why people in stable relationships indicate a greater sense of happiness than their more free-floating contemporaries. That is why a separation or a loss stirs such deep-seated anxious feelings in our guts that are so difficult to dispel or control. Aloneness has always spelt greater danger for mankind than connectedness, and we feel that in our bones.

First Religious Ideas
Another way of assuaging the Big Fear has been religion in one form or another. It is assumed that the first form of religious thinking developed with the Neanderthal men, a species of homo

sapiens that lived in Northern Europe at around between 180.000 and 60.000 BC.

The Neanderthals were a peaceful tribe, hunting and gathering and developing skills and tools to make their life easier. It is believed that they lived in harmony with their surroundings and for that reason have not left many traces. Whatever "litter" their lifestyle produced, was reintegrated and recycled. They had learned to use every bit of the animals they hunted and their tools, made of wood and stone, were used and passed on, until they disintegrated.

What traces they did leave behind, however, gives us an indication that they were among the first to practise certain burial rituals. Before this, humans who died were probably simply left behind, as if something unknown and bad had happened to them. For the first time in human history, the Neanderthals seem to have figured out the inevitability of our life cycle: We are born, we die. Those two facts were, and are, the only certainties of a human life.

When a member of a Neanderthal clan died, the other members, having figured out by now that there would not be some form of coming into being again, began to bury the bodies and for the first time acknowledged death as something finite. By adding some gifts to the grave, of which we have traces, they indicated that death might be some other form of existence or that there was maybe a kind of afterlife, but which was definitely different from their earthly existence. Burying their dead means that now it was acknowledged and accepted that we are only passing by on this planet and that we are transient. It was this acknowledging of "before" and "after", of "life" and "non-life" that was new to man's thinking. Maybe the adding of gifts can be seen as an assuaging of their own sad or confused feelings. Not knowing much about the life cycle in general, nor about possible causes of death, would not exactly have contributed to a feeling of safety and comfort under the vast skies. But in the history of mankind, living in groups and developing rituals has increasingly served to steady their development and further their chances of survival.

U-Turn in the Middle Ages
From these beginnings various religious beliefs have developed. Since then it could be said that there is no human clan, tribe or group of people on this planet that doesn't have some form of belief in higher forces that can be held ultimately responsible for everything that is happening around them. Those higher forces also represent a kind of external instance for how to behave, a kind of moral code of dos and don'ts that again serves to anchor us and make us feel safer. If we have some rules, we know what to do and what not, rather than having to figure things out from day to day, depending on the event.

The assumption that there is something or someone much higher up out there who knows everything and can do and undo everything makes all that happens to us explainable: From earthquakes to droughts to envious neighbours or a stillborn child. Presumably, it was more the bad things happening that required some form of supernatural explanation: Only when negative events happen to us do we ask: "Why?" and despair when no obvious answer can be found. In phases of good fortune, when everything goes smoothly, be it the harvest, the hunt, the stock market or the simple feeling of well-being, no-one ever asks "Why?" The dread only sets in when negative events turn us to thoughts of the "Why" and "how" of our existence. Then it is automatically assumed that there is a "meaning" out there, some overriding system, and that we in our sad state haven't figured it out yet. In good times, when feeling more confident, we rather assume that *we* are the ones who give life a meaning.

So religions could develop on the fertile ground of huge ignorance about the workings of life and nature, and on the despair and fear people felt when misfortune befell them. And any particular set of beliefs, be it of a naturistic pantheon, finding god in nature, a more sophisticated set of higher beings such as in ancient Greece, or the one and only god in Judaism, Christianity or Islam, could provide people with comfort and solace in the good as well as the bad times. Religions provide an explanation for everything that happens, including the day-to-day living as a mere human in a vast universe, giving meaning where it is needed.

If all that cold, vast Unknown had been created by some higher force, now, with Higher Beings, it was suddenly finite and could be explored and made known, familiar and safe. What is known hardly ever frightens us. The world and its surroundings became an ever smaller place, with artificial but firm boundaries, like a stake fence surrounding a corral, to protect us from uncanny forces out there. The German word for uncanny, by the way, is "unheimlich", literally translated as "not at home". What is not at home and unfamiliar is threatening to us.

So, religious beliefs were developed into ever more sophisticated systems of rules and doctrines well into the Middle Ages. In these systems, Man was the centre of the universe practically ruling it, apart from the Higher Being, and with a belief that Humankind was the epitomy of creation, the feeling of safety in the Vastness Out There was as good as it got.

With the new astronomical discoveries by Copernicus and Galileo in the sixteenth and seventeenth century (which were considered heresy by the ruling Christian church, as they threatened the dogma at its core) Man was toppled from this position of presumed supremacy. If the sun and other stellar bodies were not circling around the earth but the earth in fact was only one small body circling the sun, one was suddenly as small and inconsequential again as aeons before under the night sky outside the cave. The universe was vast and infinite again. No more safety, no more secure boundaries, no more familiarity out there, no more boundaries of a unified creation, only cold space and infinite dread.

If that was the case, where was God, or any creator who would give us comfort? After they failed to suppress the new discoveries and the rapidly increasing knowledge, the religious systems tried to integrate the theory of an ever increasing empty universe with the tenets of the world as creation, the world as a finite environment in which Man/Woman is the supreme being ruled by the fear of God, not by the fear of infiniteness. That turned out tentative and at times quite irreconcilable. Ever so often, when news of a new discovery in space breaks, there are speculations whether one has finally found "traces" or "ripples" of god, as if after all somewhere far, far out there is a higher being responsible for it all.

Good Questions – no Answers

As highly developed rational beings, forever looking for patterns and systems, we feel deeply uncomfortable with a fundamental fact for which we as yet have no explanation. After the recent confirmation that our universe keeps expanding faster and faster, the first question that springs to mind is: "Where to? What actually is beyond this expanding boundary? What was it like 15 billion years ago when the whole thing started to expand?" Good questions, no answers – very unsatisfactory and deeply unsettling for many.

The Truth is Out there...

At the same time, we have to deal with these uncertainties, this vastness, this infinite void. We do that by drawing limits, concentrating on the near rather than the far, getting on with life - in other words, like Iris, we don't look up at the stars. "After all, we can't imagine, what we can't imagine. If truth is outside what our brain structure can handle, then it's the same as if there were no truth..." (Diski 1987, p. 81)

Being humans, we know that we don't know and we have to leave it at that – and sometimes this is not only frustrating, it also fills us with despair.

But enough of the universe and its implications. What does all this mean for our little selves? How do we see us? Where is our place? How valuable a being am I?

Who am I?

It is questions like that which point deeper to our core. If this should really be my only stab at life, how much do I have to achieve in order to make an impact? What sense or meaning can I give my life, and what does it say about me when I feel I don't come up to standards (other's as well as my own)? Am I worth the love I have been receiving from my parents? Am I a worthless individual if my parents have failed to love me the way they should have done – something I know deep inside me?

Just like the "bone-fear" resulting from frightening events in our early days, these are deep-seated feelings we carry around with us. Those "core-beliefs", of which very often we are not conscious at all, have nevertheless a great impact on how we respond to life situations and relationships.

You may ask at this point, what does all this have to do with my fear?

Well. It does not necessarily have anything to do with our particular fear or phobia or panic, but definitely with the way we are dealing with it. This depends to a great deal on how we see ourselves. So if we want to come to the bottom of a particular bad fear we are carrying around with us, we have to get to the bottom of our selves first, how we think and how we feel about how and who we are.

Our Core Beliefs
To track those core beliefs and values, we can try and find answers to the following questions:
- How do I see myself in the world?
- Am I a small and insignificant unit or a unique and precious human being?

- Do I regard myself as innately good with a few faults and weaknesses or am I a bad person, not worth forgiveness or love at all?
- How do I regard changes – as threatening my being or as being the essence of life itself?
- Am I fairly capable of dealing with life, or a pretty hopeless case when it comes to critical situations?
- Do I meet my own expectations?
- And what are these expectations?
- What is really important to me?

To come to fairly clear answers to all these questions, maybe it is a good idea if you take pen and paper and write a little essay about how your best friend would answer them in regard to you. It could begin like: "I have known XYZ (put in your own name here) for so many years and I think she or he is the kind of person who..."

I wonder what you come up with....

Back to Fran and Gina
Let's go back to our examples from the beginning: Fran was the woman with an acute fear of her violent ex-boyfriend who had suddenly reappeared.

Fran is considered a fairly confident person by her friends and family. By that, people normally mean that a person is not shy, feels quite good about him or herself, feels able to say what s/he thinks and simply "gets on with life"

If Fran would question and explore her core beliefs, she probably would come to the conclusion that she feels quite valuable and precious. She is aware of how she is and what she can and can't do. She feels loved by her family and friends and can accept those positive feelings towards her without unease or embarrassment. She is also confident that she normally deals with problems and crises in a level headed way, and can accept that sometimes she makes mistakes. It's not that she is overly happy about this or that mess she has found herself in over the years, but she can shrug those incidents off and move on without being mortified or feeling overly guilty.

Even though Fran knows herself as capable of dealing with critical situations, she feels intense fear, the kind that makes us shudder, freeze, and feel sick. Fran recognises these physical sensations as symptoms of her fear. But instead of interpreting them as signs of an imminent catastrophe, for her they are warning lights, putting her body on red alert in response to a real threat.

After this initial body-shock, the automatic response set in motion by the amygdala, triggered by the sight of Tom, her rational mind sets in. The first thing she does following the wave of fear is to remove herself from the situation. An old "flight" reaction underpinned by a rational thought.

Remember, she saw Tom in the High Street of her home town. Fran abandons everything she had planned to do, backs off to walk close to the shop windows on the opposite side of the street from Tom and takes the quickest way back to her car, all the while making sure that Tom has not seen her and is not following her.

Inside the car, which she locks, she takes a deep breath. Already her heart is not racing so very fast anymore, but is beating slower and steadier. Then she starts to think…

With a mind less trusting in her own capacity of dealing with critical situations, Fran might have panicked. Maybe she would have stood stock still, frozen, attracting the attention of other passers-by, and maybe even Tom's. In a panic, she may also have started actually running away, the pure "flight" response from our forefathers which, again, might have attracted attention.

Instead she took her physical warning signs – the racing heart, the sinking feeling etc. - as simply that and not as orders that her body had to follow these signs helplessly.

Her mind, alerted by the warning signs, told her to remove herself, and that's what she did. Back in a safe place, the car, she can begin to analyze the situation and ponder about strategies.

Gina, however, is considered a bit shy by her friends. Since the divorce a few years ago, she is known to sometimes "chicken out" of events or evenings out that involve a certain level of carefreeness. The other week she didn't join them for a Karaoke session in the pub, and at the big staff meeting last month she didn't get up to say something, even though her friends knew where she stood on the issue of more pay to compensate for working on bank holidays.

Deep down Gina feels guilty about her failed marriage, as if it had been entirely her fault that her and her husband couldn't agree on how to raise the children and who would look after them. This feeling of guilt, of having failed, has knocked her confidence, the "feeling good about oneself". She principally feels alone, abandoned, worthless, not really good enough. This insecurity undermines her reponses to near enough everything. With a lack of self-trust and confidence one tends to avoid situations that would call for a bit of courage, of putting oneself out, of chancing, of risk taking – and also quite normal encounters with other people

Alone or Solitary?

We are still exploring how we feel in the face of the vast freezing void out there – all alone, as far as we know. It is this fact that we somehow have to come to grips with. We need our own, individual strategies to cope with that dread – which is the

We each need our own individual strategies

flip side of the feeling that each and everyone of us is a unique and therefore infinitely precious human being. If nobody else is ever quite like us, if we are so unique, it also means that ultimately we are on our own, having to deal with whatever life throws at us. This awareness of that ultimately inevitable aloneness is probably utterly human. As all core issues - such as light not existing without darkness – aloneness has a positive as well as a negative side to it. Being alone is one of the things people fear more than anything. Man from the beginning, as we have seen, has been a social animal. One of the greatest scares in societies, whether they were tribal or sophisticated like the Roman Empire, has always been expulsion - being shunned, being driven out, being made to stand apart and left to our own devices, alone, without the comfort, support and feedback of a group. Given our herd or group instinct, we can't stand it very well to be excluded and standing on the sidelines. Especially in modern times, there is hardly any aloneness other than in this negative sense. Not following the latest fashion makes us stand apart. Not having the newest gadget, we feel left out. Not feeling courageous enough to go to the hottest club with our mates, leaves us left at home and not feeling very good about ourself.

These days we enjoy an infinite offer of distractions, entertainment, and demands to keep us from the risky state of aloneness, a state in which we might be susceptible to feelings of not just fear of something concrete, but of the more fundamental dread of being in this world.

It's Time to Accept
I think it is one thing we have to come to accept – that we are ultimately alone and that we have to face the fact of being "thrown" onto this planet, as the German philosopher Heidegger put it, and that we have to deal with this, probably our only life, as best as we can as precious and unique individuals.

As we have seen, mankind from the very beginning of conscious thinking and feeling has turned to others for comfort and solace. Only in other beings we can find ourselves. Only the social constructs of family, friends and acquaintances and our attachments to them can give us the anchoring and grounding we need so that we can bear this fundamental isolation. It's to prevent the feeling of giddiness we mentioned at the beginning of this chapter – but it is more about facing it. That's probably what Bob Dylan means in his song "I saw a shooting star, and I thought of me" (and of course, of his lover), of being ultimately alone in the vast void. My friend Iris, who felt that giddiness, managed throughout her life to create a comfort zone around her which consisted not only of her own family and relatives, but also of a large circle of friends. She found her own solace and comfort by being there for everybody and by giving them in turn solace and comfort. She kept her gaze forward and steady rather than lifting it to the shooting stars.

And that is one way of dealing with our existence. Another one is to embrace the aloneness and use it in a positive way. Only in a solitary state we can check and develop our thoughts, can we be and trust ourselves and develop our inner lives. I am not advocating for all of us now to become reclusives, but in the face of a strong emphasis on social life these days, it is important to balance it out by more time on our own. Often aloneness is considered as "unhealthy" or "antisocial", and that assumption leads to a frantic chase of any company for the sake of it. Today's life offers us easy access to people at all times – be it at the workplace, on public transport, during leisure time in the gym, or in the virtual sense in chat rooms or by communicating via phone and email.

As this takes up a huge chunk of our lives, aloneness is getting rarer and therefore scarier and is often equated with being lonely and pathetic.

But often the hectic social life leads to a great sense of emptiness and failure to "be happy" when we are supposed to feel that way, as we don't have the time to sort out our thoughts, our preferences, the way we want to live and what we definitely don't want. Only in solitude can we tell the wheat from the chaff – otherwise we tend to simply go along with what is going on at the time without much further consideration. And that is not a sure recipe for achieving happiness. Being oneself, confidently trusting in one's own values and opinions, makes us more capable of dealing with others as well as with negativity and crises – as we can see in Fran's example.

... and what about Happiness?
That leads us to the question of happiness itself – a feeling state that is potentially just as strong as fear. And as with other feeling states, the emotion precedes the consciousness. We never decide to be happy – we either aren't or we just are, and only then do we realise it consciously. It's not only as the flip side of the strong negative emotion of fear that it deserves our attention. After all, as peace is not just the absence of war, happiness is not simply the absence of dread, but rather a positive, multi-layered state of mind.

Just as there has been a lot of research on the brain and its feeling states and functions in recent years, there also has been a lot of insights into the workings and mechanisms of happiness – or of people who appear to feel happy more often than others.

It's Taking Part That Counts!
Since the Seventies there has been increasing interest not only in the maladies of our mind, but also in the aspects that make some people apparently more happy than others. The Hungaro American Mihaly Csikszentmihalyi was one of the first to thoroughly investigate the so called state of "flow". People in flow are com-

pletely immersed in what they are doing, to the extent that all other thoughts are eclipsed. Being totally focussed in that way, people unanimously report of being completely happy. Most people reach this state when they pursue a hobby, when doing their favourite activity – be it windsurfing or baking cakes – or when they are a member of that lucky group of people who enjoy their actual paid work. The less concentration we have to apply to an activity, the less well-being or happiness we gain from it. That means when we do nothing at all, our thoughts have a tendency to drift into negativity or chaos. Sweet Nothingness doesn't seem to do the trick of putting us into a state of bliss at all. Most people who have experienced phases in their lives when they were forced to inactivity – be it in hospital, unemployed, stranded somewhere, or in prison – will report that their mood deteriorated rapidly. This was not only due to distress when ill, to lack of status after the loss of a job or when sentenced to do time behind bars, or due to an actual danger when stranded somewhere, but much more so to the forced inactivity of the mind.

Mindgames

Other examples for the onset of low mood and negative thoughts can be found in the reports of people who were taken hostage and held in captivity for a long time. And in the same reports we find brilliant examples of how to overcome this lethargy of the mind which so quickly turns into despair. Excellent examples for turning critical situation around for them by using their time wisely, are Terry Waite and Nelson Mandela. They overcame the crippling state of low mood with its accompanying brothers fear and panic by forcing their minds to do some sort of work, by setting themselves tasks, sometimes imaginary ones, and to remain active in every possible way. Csikszentmihalyi describes wonderfully how people in forced isolation invented whole mind games by imagining for example that they set off on a world journey. Before their inner eye they travelled step by step, visiting places they had never really seen, by experiencing imaginary adventures and by overcoming fictitious dangers. And all the while the time passed more quickly for them, and their mood oscillated between excitement, awe, thrill and sheer bliss – all in the mind!

We can create happiness in our mind by actively taking charge

So, the less our minds are activated, the less happy we feel.
The lowest common denominator seems to be watching random television. Just sitting in front of the box and looking at some moving pictures just about keeps our thoughts from drifting into negativity – just about. For a distinctive feeling of happiness we simply have to do more – at least take the first steps towards an activity – and any activity will do as long as it captures our thoughts.

Positive Psychology

More recently, Professor of Psychology Martin Seligman postulated what is now called "Positive Psychology". This very useful concept leaves behind the approach that considers the mind only in terms of its aberrations and negative expressions. Since Sigmund Freud and the development of psychology, the science of the mind has concentrated on what goes wrong for us – whether we call it hysteria, "the nerves", depression or, more recently GAD – general anxiety disorder. This, in tandem with a vast offer of various pharmaceuticals to make it better, was what psychology, psychiatry and analysis was about so far: We have to weed out the negativity in our minds in order to be happy or label the various negative states and develop some medication. This didn't really work – considering that one in four people suffer from some negative mind disorder at some point in their lives, and that an equally high number of people in the Western world is more or less continuously on antidepressants. Pills at best camouflage the symptoms of unhappiness and make us just about tick over. They sometimes prevent us from looking at the underlying state of our mind and what can be done about that.

Rather Look on the Bright Side

For the last five years Seligman has encouraged fellow psychologists to study what goes right in people's lives rather than what goes wrong. By getting to know better what makes people tick, what gives them a feeling of fulfilment, he aims at figuring out how to build a feeling of strength and well-being in people.

Focus on what goes well, what makes you tick and what makes you feel fulfilled

---

He feels that, particularly in this age of consumerism and heavy advertising, armies of unhappy people are created who are well aware of the fact that most things on offer these days are not attainable for them. The satisfaction of artificially created needs for ever more comfort and labour saving devices, for entertainment and kicks doesn't really make for happier people. What is created is more of a void, an emptiness that no amount of gadgets can fill. Being happy, it seems, gets more and more difficult for us.

Three Ways to a Happy Life

Seligman figured out that there are three basic ways of living to achieve happiness in one's life. The first is the "Pleasant Life" – which means satisfying the physical needs and to create visceral pleasures. Happiness is a nice hot bath, a good meal with some wine and other creature comforts. These kinds of pleasures are not very long-term, but definitely give us many moments of just feeling good – if we are able to create it for ourselves.

The second way of life he calls "The Good Life" – and it reminds us of Csikszentmihalyi's Flow-theory. The Good Life has many elements of social activities, of challenges in various areas, be it fundraising, entering competitions for salsa dancing, or playing badminton on a Sunday afternoon in the park. Doing something and focussing on it as much as possible really makes for a more durable feeling of pleasure and happiness. We feel more satisfied with our selves, our stamina, with being cherished as a friend, or as a valuable member of the community. Those things are longer lasting in our minds than the pleasures of the body described above.

The third way of living a happy life is called "The Meaningful Life" This, according to Seligman, gives us the highest level of sustained happiness. Caring for others, engaging in politics, working for a voluntary organisations not only keeps our thoughts and bodies occupied and focussed in flow, it also gives our life a meaning, a sense of why we are here. This feeling of being part of something important makes us feel good about ourselves. We have already seen how the way we feel about ourselves has an important impact on how we deal with stress and fear. Gaining positive feedback and feelings from commitments, activities and flow situations enhances our self-worth and with that the ability to deal with adversity.

Finding a meaning in your life can only happen from within

A Happy Brain

Another branch of this "happiness research" has come up with astonishing results about how mind and body interact not only in a state of unhappiness, despair or panic (we have described the physical responses of that state in detail – the sweating, the dry mouth, the racing pulse etc.). There are also strong physical responses in a state of bliss. Research on Buddhist monks with their regular practice of meditation, of clearing their mind consciously of all fleeting thoughts to reach a calmer, more peaceful state, has shown that people who follow this practice have an increased activity in the parts of the brain connected with happiness. It is as if - again, as in the circuit of fear – the neural pathways activated when in a happy state, become stronger and faster, in fact more accessible. When not constantly activated and triggered, neural pathways indeed can fur up and become much more difficult for the electric impulses that make up our thinking and feeling to travel on.

So, you may ask, what does it all have to do with my constant state of fear, of anxiety and worrying, of crippling panic attacks?

Conclusions

In this chapter we have moved from way back, about how our forefathers and –mothers dealt with the "being here", to how mankind developed systems and zones of comfort and solace in family, friends and religious systems. We ended with a description of how people function and work their lives, who consider themselves happy and who are very often sought out by others because they appear genuinely happy to them,

It seems that in order to live a reasonably satisfactory life, we first and foremost have to accept who we are and what we are doing on this planet. As said before, our minds are as complex as the universe itself and with equally infinite possibilities. We have to embrace this concept – and not shrink back in awe before it. We can well feel empowered by the thought, that for all we know, **our mind, is the most sophisticated single thing in the whole universe.**

From that it follows that it is up to us how we go about life. Due to the research of "happy" people, we also know that it takes some challenge and quite a bit of work to achieve that desirable state. "No pain, no gain" may have sounded brutal to anyone who has endured the first years of, say, piano practice under a stern teacher. But when for the first time they play a small sonata without any flaws and in their own expressive way, and consequently experience a feeling so pleasant that it is hard to forget – then all the labour is forgotten and they want to experience it again and again.

In terms of our fears – you don't find peace by avoiding life, as Virginia Woolfe said. We better face them, whether it is the actual, individually created fear of something in our bones, or the existential dread of us being all alone out there in the freezing void. Better even than facing it, one could embrace our fears and take them on as another part of our selves that simply needs managing.

Maybe we are an irrelevant and inconsequential flicker of life in total darkness - but we can still flicker brightly.

And we are principally very capable of doing that, because the mind is a most wondrous thing.

Apart from this fundamental attitude towards life itself, there are other, more practical means and methods to conquer fear and panic. We will deal with them in the next part.

---

* Baruch Spinoza, *Ethics*

Part III.

"There is no hope without fear and no fear without hope"*

– Fear and Control

Part III.

"There is no hope without fear and no fear without hope"*

– Fear and Control

It's Possible

We have seen in the first two chapters what actually goes on in our brain – or at least, what we know so far about its processes and mechanisms. In all probability, there is a lot more to explore up there. However, emotions such as fear, anxiety, phobias and dread can now be made visible and traceable and turned into impressive computer simulations, like in Professor Robert Winston's recent remarkable BBC series "The Human Mind". How marvellous it is to watch the nerve signals racing along neural paths and the little electric flashes when they hit a synapse, a nerve connection, like in a very complex pinball machine. This is how our thinking and feeling processes look like. We know now about the mechanics of it and can visualise how it happens. But of course, we as yet cannot make visible the contents of our thoughts and feelings, and whether we ever will, nobody knows.

It would be like reading each other's mind – and maybe that would not be such a desirable thing after all and would be better left to the realm of science fiction. So, we know not only what we feel, we also know how these emotions manifest themselves *physically* as feelings, and we know how these are generated in our brain. There is a vast network of neural paths in our brain connecting to a huge and infinitely flexible circuitry to have information, knowledge and memories ready and accessible in all sorts of circumstances.

We know now what thoughts look like

These neural paths are either well routed and easy, when they are ready for everyday occurrences, for routine tasks, for reflexive responses or for being on "auto-pilot". Driving to work every morning, for example, from Monday to Friday, using the same route as easily as we do is made possible by our nerve reactions running in well-oiled grooves, aided by a constantly reinforced memory.

In our brain, there is a network of Super Highways.
A and B and C roads and lots of as yet unmarked rough tracks

If we should change jobs, or if our office is relocated, we will have to find a new route to work, and for a few days we have to pay extra attention and alertness to first finding and then re-finding the way before the same automatic, beautiful routine develops, when we can anticipate every bend and turning, every traffic light and pedestrian crossing, each landmark in its turn.

So, we have a lot of old, well-grooved nerve paths, and we know that we can create new ones which of course means that we never, ever stop learning. This, in a way, changes our outlook on old age. It does not have to be the slow decline in every aspect, the unstoppable increase of forgetfulness. Even if we lived to the age of a hundred and twenty years, which scientist are predicting for us within the next century or so, we would still have, at least to a degree, a complex and infinitely flexible and adaptable network of nerve cells and connections "up there" that enables us to learn or to look at things in a different way.

We NEVER stop learning!

Other nerve paths, apart from the well-used ones and the ones we create anew, have become a bit fuzzy or overgrown. It is possible, though, to clear them again by constant use. In other words, there is no fixed road system up there, but a constant opening and closing, chopping and changing, turning and bypassing according to demand. The map of our brain has the capacity to change and be changed quite considerably. And this has important consequences for the way we consider learning – not just facts, but also new forms of behaviour.

As for the learning of facts, we mentioned earlier the example of learning Spanish at an advanced age: We know now that new learning creates new nerve paths or re-opens old, fuzzed-over ones in our brain. In order to do some new learning, we really have to find or un-clog some learning paths in our brain first before we can hope to establish some retrievable memories for the new words and grammatical structures. It is generally acknowledged that learning a foreign language after the age of fourteen is much more difficult, as if a certain window would close at that age. In the light of what we know now, it seems, however, that for an adult language learning happens in a different way: As children we acquire other languages in the same modus as our mother tongue, by parroting and absorbing the grammatical structures on a more direct "input channel". Later in life we have to create new pathways for this kind of learning, or, if some of that kind of work has been done before, unfur and open up the old existent structures. In any case: **It is perfectly possible to learn and delearn at any age!** All it takes is more persistency – either by repetition or simply spending more time on tasks -, in the same sense as when clearing a pathway through thick undergrowth by simply constantly using it. I am thinking here of the very narrow path my cats have beaten around my house: They forever attempt to get inside, for warmth and food, so they have developed the habit of circling the house on the lookout for an open window or a door left ajar. And even their small, velvety, soft padded paws have managed to mark very clearly the path they take on this perpetual journey. It seems to work the same way with our neural connections – never mind how little time we spend daily on a new routine or task – it's the regularity that matters. Constant tiny drips in the end manage to erode big rocks. So whatever your goal, stay at it in the knowledge that you'll succeed in the end!

Constant use makes a track

Our Place in the Universe

In the second part of this book we had a look at how humans deal with the fundamentals of their existence and what this means for us, how we see ourselves in an infinite, ever expanding universe. A lot of our thinking and feeling, of our emotional make-up, if not all of it, stems from there: What is our fundamental belief about ourselves and our place in life? How do we fit into the big scheme of things? Who am I – how different from every other person, and how similar to everybody else in my humanity?

How different am I, and how similar to others?

We don't normally ask ourselves deep questions like that on a day to day basis, only in times of an emotional or mental crisis, when we also question other, more superficial things. But ultimately it boils down to this. It is, after all, our own, personal choice of how we come to grips with our existence, what angle we take and how we integrate the deeply unsettling, negative feelings of ultimate aloneness into our lives. And again, as so often, it helps to look at the flip side of this: Our Aloneness is after all only another aspect of our uniqueness. When no-one on this planet is, or ever has been, exactly like us, how can we feel ultimately connected? Even in the most intimate, or closest, or most dependable relationship, there is always a residue of that ultimate aloneness. This, at times, can be terrifying - and at the same time is a very special aspect of being "us".

The Fundamental Life Force

When dealing with fear, one of our strongest emotions, our approach to how to come to grips with the exaggerated sides of it - constant anxiety and/or panic attacks, feelings of dread too strong to be easily tolerated - has to be based on those two fundamentals: the way we are, and the way we can change this. So, as negative feelings are invariably part of our lives, they have to be integrated. We cannot change this basic condition, but we can utilize and harness the power and energy of those negative feelings as much as possible.

Negative feelings such as fear have tremendous power and energy that can be harnessed

The second fundamental is that our brains are organs that are practically infinitely adaptable. It is to a great degree in our power to change the contents and functions of our brain and its output. And in the tradition of cognitive-behavioural therapy, this also means that we have the ability to alter the way we feel by influencing the way we think.

We can change the way we feel

Another fundamental assumption for our dealing with negative feelings such as anxiety, exaggerated fear, panic and phobias is that all live organisms have an innate force not to just exist, but to live well! The 17th century Portuguese-Dutch philosopher Baruch Spinoza put it like this: "Each thing, as far as it can be by its own power, strives to persevere in its being....The striving by which each thing strives to persevere in its being is nothing but the actual essence of the thing."

Sounds a bit complicated – or too simple? What Spinoza is describing is essentially the same "organismic life force" the psychologist Carl Rogers took as a fundamental for his person-centred theory of counselling. His theory is based on the assumption that each and every individual in its core or essence wants to live a more or less satisfactory life. We all strive for just that. Nobody ever says: "I feel really miserable, and I would really like to stay that way!" We all want to feel better, at least some of the time.

Rogers often told what had first triggered this core conviction of his: One day he noticed how potatoes in the cellar responded to even the smallest chink of light by sprouting white shoots for their reproduction. He observed that these shoots always grew in only one direction – towards the light. In the same way humans (and all other organisms) strive for the light, to be in a good state of well-being, to operate smoothly rather than just tick over, to be, on balance, just a step over the line to the "sunny side" of life.

We all have a "life-force" that makes us want to be better and live a more satisfactory life

---

In seventeenth century England, people flocked to see the plays of Shakespeare and other playwrights on the stage. A lot of the plays dealt with tragic, often cruel events, like "Richard II", "King Lear", "Othello", to name but a few. At the end of those more disheartening plays, the actors and musicians regularly performed a dance to lively, cheerful music. Sometimes these dances lasted up to three-quarters of an hour. The aim of it was to restore the audience to a state of happiness, lift them out of the gloom the play might have sent them into... as if happiness was the "normal" state of being for humans!

The Way We Are
So, this is how we are and want to be and we also know our potential. Being in agreement with these three fundamentals, it means, that we regard ourselves in a particular way:

- We are each and everyone unique and as such infinitely precious. There is no other individual like you or me in this equally infinite universe.
- Our brains are designed for change. It provides us with a structure at birth, not quite a blank slate, but rather a flexible blueprint. Each of its functions can be influenced, enhanced, altered - but also dismissed, neglected and forgotten.
- The brain has a practically infinite capacity for memory – conscious, subconscious and unconscious ones. It all stays "up there" in one way or another
- All humans, as well as all other organisms, even bacteria, strive for well-being. That does not mean that happiness is our natural state of mind, only that we actively strive towards it. It does not mean, however, that unhappiness or distress is not a natural way of being. It is a complementary state of mind and as such invaluable. "No light without darkness".

In terms of our emotional state, we have a strong propensity to feel out of kilter, not quite balanced. As we have stated before, our thoughts, when not focussed on something particular, inevitably tend to drift into negativity.

It's up to us to create the balance between chaos and calmness

But the urge to feel good, balanced, happy is at least as strong as this tendency towards chaos. We are constantly at work to restore or maintain this balance. This constant struggle, this balancing out - knowing our innate goal is well-being – against the state of chaos and negativity, is part of the essence of our being human. **_And we are all able to do it!_**

Those assumptions about human life imply that we might well be pretty inconsequential specks in a vast universe, but in our own environment, and in ourselves, we have a lot of power to change both – the environment and ourselves. Gaining this perspective is a precondition for changing anything that lies between us and a reasonably happy state of being. It translates into: **"I am capable of changing things for the better, because that is what I am biologically and evolutionary programmed to do."**

Back to the Cycle of Fear
Now, let's go back to the cycle of fear that we can get trapped in quite badly.

Other than the vicious cycle of:
trigger – physical responses – further panic or catastrophic thoughts – more negative physical responses,

it is a cycle that can be described as *from big to small and from small to big.*

Underlying a frightened phase can be the fundamental insecurity we all feel at times of being all alone in the world. We are ultimately alone – that is the inevitable flip side of being unique.

Under stress, all learning is impaired

It means that nobody else is like us. And not being mind readers, it means that even with so much empathy and probing nobody ever can exactly fathom what we really, really feel in any particular moment. That is why we ultimately are alone. Precious and alone.

From Big to Small and from Small to Big
So, we feel like that at times and when things are not going well, it can have quite a bad impact on us. It is a "big" emotion, this aloneness, one of the underlying fundamentals for every human life. This "big" emotion expresses itself as a feeling in every aspect of our body – down to the tiny hairs at the back of your neck that suddenly stand up and add to the sense of dread. "Feelings are the expression of human flourishing or distress, as they occur in mind and body", Damasio puts it. "Feelings are not a mere decoration added on to the emotions, something one might keep or discard. Feelings... often are revelations of the state of life within the entire organism – a lifting of the veil in the literal sense of the term. Life being a high-wire act, most feelings are expressions of the struggle for balance, ideas of exquisite adjust-

ments and corrections without which, one mistake too many, the whole act collapses. If anything in our existence can be revelatory of our simultaneous smallness and greatness, feelings are."

What all this boils down to is what we said at the beginning of this book – that fear, as a tremendous drive, has to be embraced in order to keep it in its place and under control. Only then, we can hope to tame it and continue our striving towards a reasonable state of happiness.

Reach Rock Bottom First
Sometimes this is not easy at all. Sometimes people have to reach a state that at that moment they describe as "rock bottom", as a state when things can't get any worse, when everything around them seems to collapse, and every response seems to trigger further catastrophes.

Take the fear by its horns!

David is a twenty-four year old man – he looks like a boy really, but technically and practically, he has been considered an adult for a quarter of his life. David is at that stage at the moment which he, and everybody around him, can't help describing as "rock bottom".

David lost his father when he was sixteen, at a time when he was an adolescent in his formative years, when young people start to strike out for themselves and find an identity. This very often goes hand in hand with a lot of rebellious behaviour towards the parents, especially the father. Finding one's own identity automatically means to dethrone the childhood identification with and maybe idealisation of the same sex parent. "I am me now, I don't want to be like you, Dad!" But for David, this toppling of the father statue couldn't happen: Dad died, leaving him stranded, and with a lot of guilt that he, David, with his behaviour might have contributed to his Dad's death. That's how it started. But David, at his core a very resilient and determined young lad, focussed on getting a job and threw himself into his work. He convinced himself that he was getting on with life – but at the same time, he took every kind of drug that came his way. The drug-taking had actually started much earlier and David now used them more and more to numb an emotional pain, a pain he didn't know anything about or where it came from.

Then, ten months ago, he collapsed after a night out on speed, suffered a life-threatening convulsion and was taken to hospital. He was released a short time afterwards and told to avoid drugs, otherwise he would be risking sudden death. He followed the advice and thought he was in control of things again. He looked for a job, found one and again threw himself into work. But even minor incidents caused him to lose his temper, and soon he was sacked. The same week he narrowly survived a car crash – another brush with death and again, David convinced himself that everything was alright, really, if only he kept things together and got on with his new job.

But then he began to experience panicky feelings in quite unthreatening situations and again, he didn't make much of them, as if ignoring the warning signals would make the nagging underlying feeling of dread and loneliness go away.

Then more bad things happened to him, as if under a curse: he was made redundant, and couldn't find another job for months. With just unemployment benefits, money became very short and he couldn't afford to go out much. Soon after his girlfriend left him for another man, so money was even tighter for David, as he was left behind in the rather expensive flat that he was now solely responsible for.

The only thing that kept him going for the next few months was his car. It was a sporty little motor that his mother had given to him when she had won a small sum on the lottery. David loved it, cherished it and did everything to be able to keep it on the road taxed and insured.

But there wasn't much else in his life to look forward to. The only support he had now, with very little money that didn't even allow him to eat properly, was his sister. She let him come to her flat, supplied him with some food and still managed to encourage him. His Mum had refused to take him back, not even temporarily, because she felt she had done enough for her children and was now entitled to a life of her own. This refusal had nearly broken David's heart, but he had accepted it.

The next thing was that he smashed his car – deliberately. He felt so much at rock bottom that he decided he had to part with the last thing that kept his emotions going, his beloved car. Without it, he thought, he wouldn't have anything left to care for in the world – and that would be good.

It sounds like a terrible story with a sad ending – and yet, this rock bottom situation served as a new start: The slate was wiped clean, there was acceptance that everything was in tatters, but... from then on things could only get better!

Not having anything else to care for or to look after, also enabled David to start looking at himself. Only now was he able to face his strong fears of being alone, of having had to tackle everything by himself from a very early age, of no longer even having the support of his mother.

Looking back on the disasters and mishaps that he had experienced for a period of time not only showed him that we all need a bit of luck sometimes, but also that he had a good number of personal qualities that continued to serve him well: His ambition to do well, his stubbornness to persevere, his trust that in the end things would be alright, that in spite of it all he was a good bloke. In other words: At rock bottom he was down to his core: His will to live, and not only that, but the determination to live a satisfactory life!

The negative events clarified for David, as for Fran before, his fundamental attitude towards life: being positive, combined with the will to make the most of life if given half a chance. **Do what you can as best as you can and trust that the rest will somehow sort itself out.**

The "life-force' invariably asserts itself

For Gina it was different. Remember, Gina underneath had felt very guilty about the break up of her marriage. She hardly looked at her own unfulfilled needs when the relationship went sour at all. She only focussed on her own shortcomings and failures, as if she alone could and should have made the marriage work, regardless of her partner's contribution or the lack of it.

With a more confident approach to herself and life she could have taken the view that some aspects of the relationship had failed but others definitely were worth saving and keeping to make it work in a different way. She could have valued her own input over the years and everything she still had to give to her ex-partner and her children. However, because of this presumed "failure", her trust in herself and her coping abilities had more or less vanished and left her extremely vulnerable and exposed to waves and waves of deep-seated fear of going under, of being all alone.

What could help Gina in this state of mind? It certainly wouldn't get her very far if she would train herself to balance out the panic attacks by conscious thoughts such as "It's only a panic attack and it will pass". Gina in her state of low self-esteem might even feel that she deserves to feel that awful and threatened because of her presumed responsibility for the breakdown of her marriage. With that feeling, she submits herself to the crippling attacks.

With a more balanced level of self-esteem, the thought of a panic attack being a kind of "punishment" might have made a fleeting appearance but would quickly have been dismissed by the more real evaluation of the course of her marriage. As long as Gina is beating herself up for her presumed failure, she has no firm ground to stand on to tackle the panic attacks. So, the cognitive, "thoughtful" approach doesn't help her much in her feeling state of complete powerlessness.

What could help her would be to first and foremost accept the panic attacks as a signal of her mind and her body to **accept the situation as it is.** That her body is showing signs of a fear the origins of which are not clear to her at all – but that it is there for a reason. Her panic attacks are like alarm bells to alert her to a more deep-seated anxiety.

We slowly come to a set of rules, of Dos and Don'ts that on their own or combined will help you to conquer exaggerated states of fear, anxiety or panic and lead to a more satisfactory feeling state. And this also means to go back to what we stated before: The cycle from Big to Small and from Small to Big. Remember, the Big feeling of fear, of aloneness, of panic effects us in even the smallest aspect of our life. However, we can turn things around and gradually claim back our control and achieve a state of relative happiness by going the opposite way: from Small to Big. Step by little step we will claim back our mind, our thoughts, our body from the claws of fear to arrive at an equally embracing feeling of well-being.

The following Dos and Don'ts represent those steps. Remember, **you are your own best expert**. It is up to you which ones of the suggested thoughts and responses are working for you and which ones don't seem to function. Try them out, once, twice, maybe three times and then decide whether or not they will find a place in your repertoire of methods to balance out your unwanted fear and panic. Discard the ones which are not working for you. Set up, maybe write down in your own note book, which responses make sense for you and have an effect on your negative feeling state.
Over to you now!

Do's and Don'ts

I. Don't necessarily stay in the situation you become fearful in.

If you feel you can follow the next few rules while staying in the same situation during a panic or fear attack, that's fine – or even better. But if you need to gain an initial boost from taking control, move!

If you have experienced panic attacks among crowds of people, say in a supermarket, on a crowded train, in a traffic jam, or on the motorway, you have probably experienced the strong urge to leave the situation: get off at the next stop, pull over to the hard shoulder or run out of the shop leaving the trolley behind.

This can alleviate the acute feeling of panic, but you most probably replace it by another negative feeling: Embarrassment or shame. Then you'll have to deal with that on top of still having to calm yourself down and to restore a state of relative positiveness.

So, if you can just about manage it, stay where you are and focus on the following. Remember Gina: She did pull over, as she was too upset to safely continue driving. There was no other option for her. Fran, however, had to leave the situation, too, but only after considerations and rationalisations had set in. She made the decision in her own best interest to remove herself from a dangerous situation, not in order to run from her intolerable feelings. Also, if you leave a frightening situation rather than riding it out, it will be more difficult the next time. If you stay, you will remember that the last time it happened you got through it without coming to any harm – which is a positive learning experience.

So, whether you remove yourself from the scene in which you are experiencing a fear attack, or you chose to deal with it there and then, it is important that you start by **accepting it as it is.**

II. Don't belittle it – it's real

The next step in accepting the fear as part of you is to remind yourself that this is a real situation you are in. It's not madness, it's not a sign of weakness, it's something you are experiencing and that is part of your personal, unique make-up. We need our emotion of fear, it's not something superfluous, annoying or something we want to get rid of for good. Fear is big, it's strong and it can be incredibly useful. Fear is not a sign of an illness or your mind going crazy. It's real. You are frightened of something at this very moment, only you're not quite sure of what. So, there is no reason for beating yourself up about it or berating yourself as being "silly". You are not silly! **You are frightened and it's okay if this shows.** So, you might as well stay where you are.

Maybe the next time you go into a supermarket and you are feeling normal and positive, take some time to take a closer look at the other customers. You will most probably find one or two that seem to have stopped what they were doing – choosing items to put them into their trolley. They appear to take time out and reflect on something. Their eyes are a bit clouded over, as if looking inwardly. Sometimes you can hear them taking a deep breath and after a moment or two start pushing the trolley again. These people might be experiencing an attack of acute fear at that very moment you are looking at them. Notice that they don't exactly look distressed. They seem to be more in a reflective state, concentrating on what is going on inside them. You know how distressing panic and anxiety feel inside yourself and that in the grip of it you have no idea of what will be happening to you the next moment. But unless you are crying, only people who take a closer look at you will notice something a bit different.

How often until now have you found yourself looking at other people in this questioning way? When we shop, go on the underground and especially when driving, we hardly ever take the time to look at others, unless something draws us to take notice. And others in turn hardly look at us unless something attracts their attention.

It is therefore quite safe to stay in the middle of a crowd and deal with the overwhelming feeling of fear there and then without drawing attention from others that might be unwanted at that moment.

Sometimes, again, it can be the right thing for you to do exactly the opposite: Your are not belittling what you are feeling - you actually show the world at large what it is like for you and make a point. David on the one hand smashed his beloved car to show himself and others around him of how he was feeling and what he was capable of - and on the other how much he was determined to change the way he felt. I'm not saying now that you should walk out of your house and do some damage. But some gesture or ritual that is not only of great significance for you but also tells other people clearly what life is like for you at that moment and what you intend to do, can be an incredibly liberating act. I know of people who have thrown away most of their old clothes to make a new start, to set a sign, to reduce their belongings to a minimum in order not to be burdened by them. Others change around the furniture in their flat, again throwing out a lot of old things in order to let new things come in. You might have experienced thoughts like that, only so far, you have not dared to take them further and act on them.

III. Don't accuse yourself of being weak

Remember what we have said about fear in the first part – that without fear we would most probably not have survived as a species. Without fear, you yourself might not survive a dangerous situation, like a fire.

A fearless person might think they can handle it: "It's only a small fire that is easily brought under control." According to all experience, even a small fire can very easily get out of hand, especially if fabrics and materials are involved that when burning give off toxic fumes. One might be able to stifle the actual flames, but still be killed from those fumes when the, say, foam-filled armchair keeps on smouldering. So showing fear and leaving the situation to alert the fire services who are better equipped to deal with this is a sign of strength, not of weakness.

Coming back to your own exaggerated, panicky kind of fear you are experiencing in most unlikely, most unfrightening situations, it's a good idea to still accept your fear as a warning signal of a kind. We have described before how Freud distinguished between automatic anxiety (of a real danger) and signal anxiety (of a presumed threat). After a trauma people often stop believing in the latter, the warning kind. For them everything is now a real danger. It's necessary to learn the difference again: Is this a real danger or just a possibility? And again, stopping to examine one's feelings about it is a sign of strength. You want to know what is going on for you. Maybe you decide you need some professional help to probe deeper for what is triggering this fear. **This is definitely not a sign of weakness. You are strong, because you are dealing with what is going on inside you!** It is a bit like with the foam-filled burning armchair, but this time it is inside you: There are no obvious flames indicating what is troubling you, but a quiet smouldering underneath that can be deadly toxic.

III. Don't think your life is in danger

In spite of what we have said before about fear being our ally in the fight for survival, it is important to know that during an attack of exaggerated fear or panic your health is not in danger. All the alarming physical symptoms you are experiencing – the rapid heartbeat, the dizziness, the stomach cramps, the profuse sweating – are the *normal* responses of our body that are triggered in the respective brain centres entirely for this purpose. Our body is perfectly equipped to endure those symptoms as they are part of a natural internal mechanism to deal with life.

As difficult as it may be to remind yourself in a panic situation that this is normal for a fear reaction, it is important for you to **steer through and bring your responses back to a more normal level.**

You will probably find your own best method for bringing the important thought that your life is not in immediate danger, back to the forefront of your mind when it is at risk of being flooded by fear. Some people connect important messages like that with an object they always have with them: a pebble they have picked up on a favourite beach, a little talisman or charm, a certain piece of jewellery. Touching the object reminds and connects them with the important message: "I'll be alright." Other people have "trained" themselves to take a certain position when they feel in danger: They fold their hand as if praying, rub the place of the "third eye" between the eyes, or curl their toes tightly.

Think of what might work for you, and try to establish a firm connection between this reminder and the important message that your life is not in danger. You will not suffocate by being breathless. You will not faint

Nobody has ever died of a panic attack.

For Gina this was a very important step on her journey to bring her life back to a more comfortable level of confidence and trust without crippling fear. She had chosen to have a small handkerchief with her wherever she went on which she regularly sprinkled some drops of lavender oil, her favourite scent. Whenever she felt a fear attack coming, like an aura, she would take out this tissue and sniff the beautiful scent. This immediately dispelled the most threatening part of the panic, the fear of death, and was an important step on her way of leaving the fear where it belonged. Using a symbol, a ritual, or a particular gesture or behaviour serves as a grounding mechanisms that enables us to get calmer, to look at ourselves and around us more clearly and to gain more of a grip on our fear.

My grounding object/ritual/gesture
....
....
....

You know from past experience, that the strong scary feelings *will* pass eventually. Generally, they last only three to four minutes.

IV. Don't fight the sensations - ride through them

By this we mean that it is a good idea *not* to fight the incoming panic by tensing even further, by following catastrophising thoughts, or by taking the physical symptoms for signs of imminent harm.

By using your own special method of acknowledging an imminent panic attack, as we have suggested above, you immediately take back some of the control you feared you were about to lose. After all, you know best when a panic attack is about to happen, and only you can take action.

After that first step, try and let the feelings wash over you and at the same time consciously take notice of them and focus on them. By that we mean to register what is going on for you and say it, just to yourself, maybe out loud. The following is the start of a list of physical symptoms during a panic attack that you might wish to continue as you experience it:

My heart is beating faster,
My palms are getting sweaty,
My stomach feels nastily cramped
....
....
....

By focussing on the physical feelings, you avoid letting your thoughts go the way of: "I feel horribly threatened, and frightened, I'm going to die!" You are taking up the reins again and gain more control.

Further control can be achieved by not just noticing the physical symptoms (which in itself already detaches you from the worst impact), but at the same time by evaluating and grading them: At worst, the physical expressions of a panic attack reach ten out of ten on an imaginary scale. You can slowly gain more control by first distinguishing the different symptoms and look at them one by one, and then also by judging how strong they appear to you this time: The stomach feelings are 8/10, I'm sweating profusely, that is more like 9/10. My heart is already beating slower and it's going down, to 7/10 ... and so on.

For Gina it was a very important step, that, after the initial gesture of taking out her handkerchief and inhaling a few deep breaths of her favourite scent, she focussed on her body. For her it was the first time that she practiced this "inward" look to register what was going on for her, so initially it was not easy. As she was always anxiously looking at other people around her, be it in the family, at work or in public places, wondering whether she might be judged by them, she had never consciously noticed what was going on inside her. Until the day when these neglected feelings, as expressions of her inner deep emotions, erupted in a full blown attack.

At first tentatively, then with more and more knowledge of what was going on inside her, Gina began to take notice of how her body reacted. Initially she experienced her symptoms, when she looked at them one by one, as very frightening, triggering thoughts such as: "Will my heart stop beating because it is racing so hard now? Will I die younger because my heart is getting worn out by this? Is there something seriously wrong with my stomach to make me feel like that?"

Gradually, by focussing on them, the symptoms of her fear became more familiar, and she soon managed to take notice of them in a more detached way: "My hands are sweating, but I can dry them on the tissue in my coat pocket." And watching her heart from initially racing wildly to slowly calming down again, all the time focussing on it and grading it, in the end actually became a positive experience. It actually made her feel quite proud of what this, what Woody Allen called "the most flexible little muscle" was capable of.

Another way of "riding out" the negative physical symptoms of an acute fear or panic attack is to visualize them. By that, we mean to create or choose an image in your mind that most resembles what is going on for you in your body. Some people compare the onset of a panic attack with the eruption of a volcano. At first it grumbles and shakes (the pulse starting to race), then smoke breaks out (the sweat), the mountain bursts open (we might start shaking and go light-headed) and everything goes up in the air. Then things slowly fall down and settle again. After a volcano eruption everything is different – shapes have altered, rocks are not in the same place – and yet the landscape is fundamentally the same. After a panic attack you feel differently, because after all, you experience it differently every time, and yet afterwards it is still you, with your unique inner landscape and your will to live in an alright way.

Other people like to compare a phase of acute fear with a storm at the seashore. The wind (the increasing heartbeat) gradually whips up the waves until they threaten to flood you. You feel in real danger but you can retreat to a safer place and watch how the waves decrease in size and ferocity by and by until they have reached a comfortable level again when you can enjoy their incessant coming and going and actually can consider it as soothing.

Find your own unique way of visualising what is going on for you. What does this state remind you of – what does it most feel like? Is it all bad – or does it have elements you can actually quite enjoy as they give you a thrill? Notice also how the state of acute anxiety decreases after a fairly short time. Tell yourself this by grading the symptoms, as described above, until you feel you are back to what is normal for you. Don't forget, you are still you!

My own visualisation:
....
....
....
....

V. Concentrate on your breathing

Another effective way to ride out an attack of acute fear is to concentrate on your breathing. Very often, in a tense situation, we actually forget to breathe properly, and only when getting short of breath, we take a big gulp of air to get the oxygen supply going again. Notice what you tend to do when you are getting tense. Try and breathe out more than in – that way you automatically empty your lungs which in turn makes you take in more fresh air. **Breathing more out than in also calms you down.** You can actually enhance the experience by saying "CALM!" when you breathe out. It sounds a bit like sighing when you do this, and maybe it is a good idea to see it like that: Your are distressed after all, and this is a way of showing it - to yourself and maybe others.

You can easily try out the effect of breathing more out than in when you do the opposite: Take a few deep breaths one after the other, without breathing out too much, and notice how your body responds to it. Is your heart beating slower or faster? Do you feel more alert ore more relaxed? We can use conscious breathing to different effects: Breathing more out than in makes you feel calmer, more in than out makes you more awake, more alert, more ready for action. And what you want to do in an already peak alert situation of your body is clear: **Your aim is to calm down and to take control.**

In tandem with taking more control of your breathing, focus on how every part of your body feels. This is different from the concentrating on how your symptoms feel for you – the heart, the skin, the stomach - as we described in the paragraph before.

Now we want to actually look at the whole body, starting at the very bottom, with our toes. Have we curled our toes involuntarily, as our body has tensed up as a response to being flooded by fear? If that is the case, curl them even tighter! Count to four and hold very, very tight. Then slowly, again, if you can manage it, on the count of four, let the muscles in your toes go, go, go. They will relax, and feel warmer, heavier ... relaxed.
You can repeat this focussing/relaxing exercise with your whole body, gradually working your way up from the feet to the head.

At first, it may be quite difficult to locate the exact muscles that we so automatically tense up when flooded by a threatening emotion. Maybe it is an idea to practise it in a state of relative calmness, maybe when going to bed at night. Lying flat on your back helps to achieve the feeling of loosening up, of sinking into the mattress, of feeling heavy and relaxed – after we have tensed particular muscles or groups of muscles for a few seconds.

Starting at the feet, you work your way up through the legs. Tense your the calves muscles and let them go, then the area around the knees. Clench your thighs, then the buttocks ... and let go. Tense your back, the stomach and so on further up your body, every time counting to four for holding, and to four - or more if you wish - for letting go completely. All the time your mind will have to concentrate on particular muscle groups and how to tense and relax them. Don't forget your shoulders, your jaws, your tongue. Are you frowning? Relax your forehead.

And again, **you are your own best expert of your body, only you really know how to do it, and you are able to find your own best approach or method to achieve this kind of relaxation.**

VII. Do something repetitive

So far you have concentrated on your body and on your perception by looking inward, and on your environment by looking outward. You have taken control in your mind by assessing what was going on. You have taken conscious choices of whether to stay or to remove yourself from a threatening situation. **You have exercised control.**

If you feel ready, now it's the time to try out doing something that might lead you away from the feelings of fear and panic. Doing something repetitive can further help to calm you down and ease you over to a state of normality.

If you are in a public space, you can start walking, but in a controlled way. Take ten or fifteen steps into one direction, then turn round and either change direction or go back. Count your steps. Focus also on what is going on inside your body and mind. Walk. Breathe. Count. Repeat the exercise until you get the feeling that you have released some of the high energy that fear gives you (for a very good reason, but you don't need it now).

Another way of discharging energy is, if you happen to be at home, start to tidy up your space. Some people find the sorting and shifting of our day to day clutter very therapeutic in any case, so maybe it helps you, too. Put everything away that has been lying around. Have a look at your wardrobe and chest of drawers whether your clothes need some sorting out. Throw away or recycle what is not really needed. Taking control of your environment and creating it in exactly the way you would like it to be can significantly contribute to gain back a feeling of control and calmness. Another reward is inbuilt in this exercise, that at the end of it you can settle down in a perfectly calm and tidy and beautified space to relax.

VIII. Ground yourself

Now, what do we mean by that? A grounding activity is something that brings us in close touch with practical reality, with the actual world around us in contrast to what is going on in our head and how we perceive our environment.

When in the grips of a panic attack, thoughts are swirling around in our head like leaves in a hurricane. All connections to what life is normally and really for us are being swept away. We feel confused, don't know even how to start thinking straight. We fear we are losing our grip.

Grounding means, to bring us back into contact with life as it is – with the facts, the structures, the reality around us, in short, with the hardware rather than with the software in our heads that has gone a bit funny.

We have already mentioned some ways of re-connecting with the outside world: Choosing a symbol, a gesture or ritual can bring us back and ground us again. Gina, apart from having chosen a particular scent to connect her, also liked to assume a certain body posture: If the situation allowed it, she would sit down, with a straight back, and place both feet firmly on the ground, as if wanting to be in close contact with the earth. This way she felt she could counter the floating, disconnected sensation and the light-headedness in her head.

Some people find it very helpful to eat something, be it a sweet, a mint, or any other light snack. If you fear of being overwhelmed by a panic attack at any given moment, it might be a good idea to have something to eat or suck in your pocket or handbag. And as described above, to focus on the physical sensation of eating, chewing, swallowing, or sucking can take your thoughts away from the racing, negative messages that might flood your mind.

I have once witnessed how a desperate young man who was suffering from an acute psychosis and knowing that something was not quite right for him, struggled for several hours to keep his mental balance. His way of grounding himself again, of earthing himself to the world as he knew it to be reliable, rather than giving in to getting lost in the threatening, swirling chaos in his head, was to eat, eat, eat. At first he went out and bought two Chinese takeaways which he methodically finished off down to the last grain of rice. After that, still in the grips of frightening feelings in his head, he ate seven oranges, methodically peeling one after the other, carefully removing even the slightest bits of white from the segments, and then, one by one, he ate them slowly. As long as he was doing this, he felt reasonably safe. All the while he was also discussing what he was feeling inside, debating what was real and what was not, checking it out with his listener, and it helped him to a degree not to completely lose control

This was an incident with a seriously mentally ill person – and panic attacks are not a mental illness, they are a temporary state of being out of control, being flooded by otherwise normal mechanisms of fear and dealing with danger. But the approach, the method of dealing with such a state, the "grounding" is similar – finding something that is known, familiar and reliable. It is like **finding an anchor on which you can safely hook your sense of normality.**

So, focussing on a "normal" activity such as eating something, sitting straight with your feet firmly placed on the ground, or having a glass of water can help you to stay "anchored". Whatever is your choice of "anchor" – and you might have other ideas what might work for you - reflect on what you are doing and keep your thoughts as focussed on it as possible.

My choice of anchor:
....
....
....

IX. Be in the Present

This is another very practical approach for when you feel being swamped by uncomfortable feelings and sensations. It means to focus on what is actually going on this very moment. Try not to go back into the past. Pondering what went wrong, where you might have failed, what other people have done to you won't help you now. Don't stray into the future either – by imagining what might happen, what other people might say about you, whether you will be able to carry on and such like is equally unhelpful.

Stay in the here and now. We have already described how you can make inroads into the cycle of fear by focussing on what is going on in your body. You take notice of your heart and the pulse, your breathing and how to slow it down, and whatever else is going on for you that is out of kilter. The next step was to concentrate on your body in general, which muscles you were tensing up, and how you could, by and by, gradually relax your whole body after clenching the muscles hard.

The next way of turning towards "normal life" again is directing your focus on your immediate environment. Where are you? What is going on around you? Are other people present? Has anybody noticed that you are not quite yourself at this moment? If you are somewhere in a crowded place chances are, that nobody has paid any attention to how you are right now. Try and focus your thoughts on the outside now, rather than your inside. Are you sitting or standing comfortably and firmly grounded? Is it safe where you are? Do you feel like talking to somebody, ringing a friend, or do you want to attempt a chat with the lady at the checkout?

After only a short time of doing this, you will feel how the physical symptoms that can be so terrifying slowly fade away. Now it maybe the time to turn inwards again to check and grade your physical sensations. This confirms to you that the acute phase is over and that you can enhance this by starting further relaxing activities – such as breathing slower or visualising how the flood is ebbing away. You are slowly regaining control again

When Gina had pulled over to the hard shoulder, at first she was so shaken by her sobs that she was not able to even think of any of the approaches that might ease her out of that state. Supported by her work-mates, she gradually felt able to calm herself down by breathing more slowly from the depth of her stomach. Being in company helped her to let go what she was feeling by talking about it. At first, she could only say a few words, naming the feelings. By and by she managed also to describe what she was doing to counter the panic – accepting it as part of her basic fears, how she could ground herself by adopting a certain posture and having a few sniffs of her lavender scented tissue.

Gradually she took in the situation, that the group was actually on their way somewhere. All in all, it only took fifteen minutes for Gina to recover from the dreadful feelings well enough that they could actually continue the journey. Gina stayed in the driving seat, even though her colleagues offered to take over, but Gina felt that focussing on the traffic and the road would help her feeling more in control and competent. She was wise enough to choose the option that would actually boost her confidence.

Again we could describe the whole process as a cycle from big to small and small to big: First the big all-round feeling swamping our body down to the last toenail. Starting from there, by and by regaining mental and physical control again so we can develop a new all-round sense of feeling alright about ourselves.

In the first nine suggestions of how to counter an acute, exaggerated sense of fear and panic, we have concentrated on how we can gain a bit of control back over our physical responses by consciously focussing on how we feel and then how to gradually try to alter this. It boils down to "mind over matter" – meaning that the mere thought of that we are able to influence how we feel and experience actually has a positive, balancing impact on our state of mind. It may take a bit of practice to establish a kind of routine of looking at ourselves, but bearing in mind what we have said of our brains before, we can do it, and with time, it becomes much easier. We have to regard these guidelines as small stepping stones on an overall path to more wellbeing and "normality" in a particular kind of situation when we are overwhelmed by fear.

Mind over matter does work

The next set of guidelines and suggestions concentrates more on general, overall aspects of our lives, not just the fear ridden situations. What can we do in general that our life becomes more suitable to our needs? It is a kind of "Aftercare Plan" when we have taken our first steps towards managing situations in which our fear is out of control. In order to do that, we have to first find out what our needs in any particular situation are – and not especially in a situation which is riddled by fear and panic and deep insecurity.

Look at your needs in general

Most probably, your needs in any situation life throws at you will be that you somehow and more or less feel in control of it. This means, you have a sense of being able to deal with it without feeling too threatened or insecure to come up with a satisfying response easily. Most likely you feel a panicky feeling creeping up on you when you are uncertain about a situation, when you're not quite sure what is expected of you or how people see you.

What situations will most likely make you feel panicky?
....
....
....

You probably know equally well that you have "mastered" situations of all kinds. At times, you have met new people without feeling shy and self-conscious. You can remember moments in which you have felt "on top of things", easy, comfortable and just "yourself"? What was it that suddenly made situations or encounters smooth and easy without giving you unpleasant feelings of insecurity, feeling threatened or fearing to fail? If you can remember situations like that, focus on them and try to figure out what elements made them easy for you.

Situations I can remember in which I have felt in control – What elements helped me towards that?
....
....
....
....

If you can't remember any situations like that at this point, just skip to the next set of guidelines that can help to lead you out of the fearful state.

When focussing on the two types of situations (comfortable and uneasy ones) you might have found an element that is present in the first and lacking in the second one: A kind of sense of your self, a more or less solid knowledge of who you are and what your strengths and shortcomings are. When you are pretty certain of being a particular kind of person – not necessarily fantastically good or academically outstanding or any such positive extremes but alright on average and "good enough" for most – it helps to feel accepted in a majority of situations and encounters. When reflecting on the kind of situation in which you most likely will feel panicky and fearful/anxious, you might have noticed that feelings and thoughts in connections with yourself will have been on the negative side, such as in: "I felt everybody was more clever/better dressed/confident etc. than me", or "I felt I was messing up again", or "Everybody was looking at me and thinking ... (nothing very positive, I'm sure!)"

And if you could remember situations in which you have felt at ease and comfortable – you might now spontaneously add "...with myself", because that is the crucial point for both kinds of situations: The sense of who you are, and that you are basically an alright person. People so easily say that "nobody is perfect" when they want to apologize for something or are making allowances for somebody else. And yet somehow we are driven by inner demands to be just that, perfect, as if perfection (whatever that is in a person!) would be the only possible way to be in a tricky situation. The truth, however, is that "alright" and "good enough" is and always will be sufficient – for the others. It is a good idea to make it good enough for us, too, to be good enough.

A life that meets our needs

Now let us go back to pathways out of situations in which we feel overwhelmed by fear and panic. We have said that with the kind of "aftercare" thoughts following this we will concentrate on issues that make our life more suitable to our innermost needs: the need to be accepted and the need to be in control of our lives.

X. Go back to what you were doing before
You have experienced a frightening attack of being overwhelmed by fear and you have panicked. The most threatening thoughts have swirled around in your mind. You have slowly, bit by bit, regained some control over the way you feel, the way you are thinking and behaving. You know that the worst is over, but you are still shaky. The next step for you may be scary: Having just experienced that you can be a person who at times is not in control, who would say that the same thing could not happen again straightaway? Going back to what you were doing before it happened may seem impossible, as if it was exactly this situation that

triggered the fearful state. Your confidence, which is not exactly strong at best of times, has taken another blow. You may feel that people are not only looking at you but are also judging you in a negative way.

As we all know fear very well, nobody judges you for being fearful

---

But then again... You have just ridden out one of the most frightening states of mind we can be in: acute fear. With acute fear our mind and body respond to real, physical danger to our lives. In a way, both your mind and your body have responded as they should. You have recognized, however, that this natural state was out of place as there was no acute danger to your life, that your fear response was out of proportion and had to do with something else rather than say an attack by a wild animal or an armed robber.

After recognizing this, you have done everything you possibly could to counter the strong and frightening feelings. You have slowly, by focussing and concentrating and, most of all, by tolerating and riding out the fear, gained control of your responses again, and the physical reactions have calmed down.

Your pulse is near normal now, the sweating has subsided, your thoughts are calmer and much more rational than before. You have brought yourself to do some calming and relaxing exercises, again accompanied by taking mental control of the situation. You have grounded yourself and have used your resources that you know would help you.

Haven't you coped brilliantly?
So, here you are – ready to go back to what you were doing. Sometimes people at this point don't feel as undermined and shaky as described above, they actually feel a sense of relief. They have - again – coped well, they know even better now that these phases do pass, and that the symptoms don't leave lasting damage to their body and mind.

It's over, and you know you can cope!

What were you doing before the panicky feelings started to flood you? Very often these attacks happen in a situation with lots of people around you, such as the supermarket, a jam-packed underground train, a fully booked workshop or seminar, so picking up were you left off might be quite easy, as in crowds symptoms of the single person often go unnoticed, as everybody is focussed on something else.

Give yourself a few minutes of time, together with some patience and care before you get fully back into the swing of things.

XI. A bit of stretching…
But before you are joining in with whatever was going on around you before, take a few seconds and do a bit of mental and bodily stretching. It will help you to do two things at the same time: relaxing and alerting your mind and body.

The human body has many automatic responses, one of them being the physical symptoms of fear that are triggered in our brain by something we perceive from the outside world. But we have talked enough of the racing pulse, the tightness in chest and tummy and so on for the time being. Another one of those automatic responses is that we yawn when we are tired – be it physically or mentally. Furthermore, this yawning is also catching. When somebody near you yawns, so will you after a few seconds. And furthermore, when you even think of yawning, you will have to do it. It is an involuntary act, this yawning. You might be able to fake it, but you can only really do it, when it comes to you – either when you are tired, when triggered by somebody else's yawning, or when you think of it… Are you yawning yet? If this has worked for you now, try it out when you feel you need some calming relaxation after a draining panic attack. Yawn as intensely as you can make it, and at the same time, depending on your surroundings, stretch your limbs and joints. Loosen up. Let go all the tension and fear.

Loosen up by yawning and stretching

Now, as a further little step on your way back to normality, smile. It is said that the mere act of exercising our facial muscles to form a smile releases certain substances in our brain that contribute to our well being.

Smile consciously. Try and think of something that makes you laugh. Exercise control over your mood and nudge it further to a state of feeling alright. **You can do it, as you are physiologically programmed to do this.**

After those first steps towards more "normality" that are still closely connected to the state of fear and panic that you experienced, we will now broaden our outlook and consider more your life in general and how you might want it to be.

As de-cluttering your wardrobe and drawers may have helped you to regain a sense of control over your surroundings and at the same time helped to calm you down, de-cluttering your life will have the same effect in a more general sense. Here, we won't look at what items of clothing or objects are no longer needed, we will look at circumstances, habits, and also people that are taking away more of our life quality than they are presumably adding to it.

XII. De-stress your life
This advice is not something to practice in a particular situation, be it in an acute fear attack or during the aftermath of it. It is meant as a general guideline to look at your life in order to identify possible stressors in it that at times might contribute to your feeling out of control with fear. And again, you can follow a cycle from small to big and big to small. Maybe, for example, you identify the lack of time in your day-to-day routine as a major stressor, as this makes you feel rushed and pressured all the time, unable to relax in any situation. You then will have to break up your daily routines into very small portions in order to find out where you can make cuts to create more time.

Do something of your choice!

Altering a small part of your day, such as more time in the morning between getting up and leaving the house/starting to work will increase your sense of wellbeing and control for at least the next few hours if in the time gained you do something by choice. This could be a series of exercises, such as yoga, having a healthy breakfast, or a short walk around the block. You choose what you will do. Doing something by choice will make a significant difference to your feeling of being rushed from one "I must do" to the next "I should" because it's you who is in control! A small thing with a big impact on the whole system.

Give yourself more choices

Try and take some time to reflect on your day to day life. What situations make you feel more frazzled, irritable, under pressure. Is there anything you can do about it – because it's only you who knows about it, and only you who can take control of it. If you don't take steps to balance your life out, nobody will. Discuss it with your friends or partner by all means, but it's down to you in the end to decide and to do it.

Only you can make changes

Remember Gina and her relationship with her ex-husband and children. They had an arrangement that had worked fairly

---

* Note: You might find it easier to identify these stressors when you look at the things that you think you "ought to do", "should do", or "must do".

smoothly for a number of years: The two children lived with their dad during the week and came to Gina's house for weekends.

When Gina looked at possible stressors in her life, it occurred to her that she very often felt irritable and under pressure shortly before the weekend. As the children only spent time with her at weekends, somehow she felt under pressure to suggest or arrange something special every time they came when all she really wanted was to spend some "normal" time with them. She was able to pinpoint the moment when anxious thoughts started to swirl around in her head: Thursday night, when she began to make plans for the weekend together. Once this was identified, she could convince herself that all she needed to do was getting enough food in for the weekend and let things take their course. Whether they would do something special or not could be decided together. It was not solely Gina's responsibility anymore. This was just a small shift – but with a major impact. The first weekend when Gina consciously kept herself from trying to make detailed plans, she and the children spent some very relaxed time at home together. They simply played and had meals together and talked about things that mattered to them without having to "schedule" all this in.

Small things that maybe are big stressors in my life*:
....
....
....
....

XIII. Develop positive statements
In a way, this could be your own summary of what you have

learned in this book. We have talked about the different ways we are – as individuals as well as humans in a general sense – and also about what we all have in common. We have learned what makes us tick, how our brain functions, and what we can do to influence both.

Looking at our lives and its stressors has given us a further perspective of how we want to be and how we want to live. We all want to be reasonably happy and free from exaggerated fear. We want to be able to communicate with others without feeling uncomfortable. We want to be ourselves and be accepted by others just as we are.

You will remember what we said about the constantly changing network of A and B and C roads in our brain, and that sometimes we have to clear some neural pathways by constantly using them, so that we can establish some new learning process – **for which it is never too late!**

We can make use of this knowledge and actually learn how to feel better about ourselves by developing statements that, when constantly repeated or used, will be integrated into our thinking and so will make a difference to the way we feel.

Positive statements make a difference to the way we feel

Again, only you can do it. Only you know exactly how you want to live and what it takes to get there. We could make numerous suggestions now and never really hit exactly what you would need to tell yourself in order to feel better. That is the reason why we only give a general guideline for this kind of positive statement: The emphasis is on the fact that you and everybody else are unique and precious beings. Without you, any situation you encounter would not be the same. You are irreplaceable. With all your weaknesses and strengths, on balance chances are that you are alright and good enough by anybody's standards.

It's up to you now to develop the positive statements along these lines that will give you the confirmation and the strength to take control in situations which otherwise threaten to overwhelm you.

Encouraging, positive statements I can give myself in a difficult situation:

....
....
....
....
....
....
....

XV. Make sense of your life

At this point of the book we have come quite a long journey: Our starting point was a look at fear as one of our oldest companions, a feeling that has been with us since the beginnings of mankind and beyond, and is known to every human being on this planet.

Then we had a good look at what at this stage is known about the physical conditions underlying this fear. What is going on in our brain when we not only feel this sensation, but also are acutely aware of its physical manifestations. We have an idea now what goes on in the centre of our brain, in the small organ amygdala, on what nerve paths the input travels and what this input triggers once it is very quickly processed in the amygdala and the thinking part of the brain, the neo cortex.

Then we had a look at a more fundamental kind of fear, the kind of dread that fills many people once they start looking at their own place in the universe. This last item of our list of Dos and Don'ts is a kind of continuation of this question: Who are we and how do we make sense of the life we have been thrown into? How do we see ourselves and our place in the immediate surrounding of family and friends, country, planet and cosmos?

Who and where are we in this?

These are questions that we don't ask ourselves very often or in a day to day conversation, but the answers are underlying our very being and are vital for our emotional state. With a pessimistic viewpoint, for example, by seeing us as completely unimportant beings, struggling to simply get through life without any good expectations, many people tend to feel a kind of big void inside them. Their need of being meaningfully attached, of belonging, of having a sense of what they are doing and what impact they are having on others, remain unfulfilled.

We have a need to feel attached, to belong

In some ways this was underlying Gina's unhappiness and anxiety. Due to her feelings of guilt because of the failed marriage, she saw herself as rather unimportant person who, at best, had a negative influence on others and very low expectations of being valued. During therapy Gina learned to focus on the positive impact she had on her children who loved her very much, and also on her husband who, in spite of the past conflict, appreciated her reliability and her commitment to remain a good parent for their two boys. Gina's feeling of being insignificant decreased considerably, together with her anxiety – which in her case was also the guilt-ridden expectation that something really bad was going to happen to "punish" her. Her fear had become a general state of mind reflecting her low expectancy of life's goodness.

Fran, on the other hand, had a solid sense of life in principle being good and of her playing an important part in her surroundings. She was certain of her commitment to her partner and young daughter, to her family and friends, and equally certain of those others feeling more or less the same towards her. "Life is give and take", she would sometimes say, meaning that life is not all sweet and beautiful, but has its trials and tribulation to be tackled or endured in the knowledge that things change all the time. It also reflects that we all give a lot without much questioning, and that it is perfectly alright to receive back.

Keep the balance between giving and receiving

For most people it probably is somehow difficult to pinpoint where exactly they are on this spectrum between "pessimistic" and "positive towards life". One way of finding more certainty about ourselves would be tracing of how we respond to situations and events. This tracing could be made easier by keeping some sort of diary. By writing down at the end of your day what has had an impact on you and in what way, you would very quickly discover a pattern. Maybe you find that changes of every kind make you feel very anxious and reluctant – maybe you'll find that new aspects and possibilities make you feel enthusiastic. What do your more frequent reactions say about you? Do they reflect a more general inner attitude – and is it in your best interest? Are you happy with your responses? Is there maybe a possibility that you could change them? Find your own pattern of recording how you feel from day to day, and maybe share your insights with a friend or partner.

Find your pattern of responding

Another way of finding out where you stand on the big question "Who am I?" is having a look at the books and films that you have read and seen over the last few years and what you remember of them as having had an impact on you You may be surprised to find that you clearly remember many details that seem irrelevant whilst having forgotten important aspects altogether, such as the plot or the ending. What do those remembered snippets say about you? Is it that you could identify with these details? Did they trigger a feeling of repulsion or horror? Would they stand for an ideal that you are trying to pursue? Only you can give the answers to these questions – and make sense of them.

These are just two examples of how to come to a clearer picture of how you are seeing yourself in this life? Both are about recording aspects of your life and thoughts that are triggered by certain experiences. And maybe you respond to this now by saying: "Isn't it selfish to be centering on myself to such an extent? Isn't this unproductive navel gazing?"

I am not suggesting that you spend your entire time now on the exploration of every aspect of your self and completely neglect your children, partner, parents and friends. It is rather about taking some time for yourself. If you don't consider yourself important, other people might find that difficult, too. With a deeper knowledge of yourself both as an individual and as a human being, you automatically gain more insights into other people's minds as well. And what could be more satisfying than not only being at more ease with yourself but also with the people around you.

If you are still reluctant to put your thoughts on paper in a regular way, make a start in this book and see how it feels…What you come up with can be the basis of your own "First Aid Kit" for tackling difficult and fearful phases in your life. The reflections about yourself alone will contribute to a greater sense of being you, and being calmer.

I wish you luck on this difficult and most interesting journey.

Afterword

I am looking out of my window. A blackbird is perched on the highest branch of the tall ash tree in front of the house. A strong gust of wind shakes it violently to and fro. The bird clings on. Does it feel fear? Maybe. And if it does, it seems to go with it, swinging to and fro and relying on its ability to ride the storm out and survive it. Maybe it is even enjoying the thrill of the situation…

Bibliography

Black, Harvey: <u>Amygdala's Inner Workings. Researchers gain new insights into this structure's emotional connections.</u> In: The Scientist, 15(19):20, Oct. 1, 2001

Birkett, Dea: <u>I know just how you feel.</u> In: The Guardian, Sept. 3, 2002

Böhmer, Otto A.: <u>Sternstunden der Philosophie. Schlüsselerlebnisse grosser Denker von Augustinus bis Popper.</u> München: Beck, 1994

Csikszentmihalyi, Mihaly: <u>FLOW: The Psychology of Optimal Experience.</u> New York: Harper & Row, 1990

Damasio, Antonio: <u>Looking for Spinoza. Joy, Sorrow and the Feeling Brain.</u> London: Heinemann, 2003

Diski, Jenny: <u>Rainforest.</u> London: Penguin 1987

Gadamer, Hans-Georg: <u>Wahrheit und Methode.</u> Tübingen: Mohr, 1960

Garland, Caroline (Ed.): <u>Understanding Trauma. A Psychoanalytical Approach.</u> Second, enlarged edition, London: Karnac Books, 2002

Holt, Doug: <u>The Role of the Amygdala in Fear and Panic.</u> www.serendip.brynmawr.edu/bb/neuro/neuro98, 2002

Huizinga, Johan: <u>Homo Ludens. A Study in the Play Element in Culture.</u> London: Paladin, 1970

Jeffers, Susan: <u>Feel the Fear and Do It Anyway. How to Turn your Fear and Indecision into Confidence and Action.</u> London: Random House, 2002

LeDoux, Joseph: <u>The Emotional Brain. The Mysterious Underpinning of Emotional Life.</u> London: Orion Books, 1999

Mahoney, Elisabeth: <u>Panic Now.</u> In: The Guardian, May 24, 2002

McKie, Robin: <u>Now science tells us how we really feel.</u> In: The Observer, March 10, 2002

Rose, Jacqueline: <u>On Not Being Able to Sleep. Psychoanalysis and the Modern World.</u> London: Chatto & Windus, 2003

Rowan, Don and Eayrs, <u>Caroline: Fears and Anxiety.</u> Harlow: Longman House, 1987

Storr, Anthony: <u>Solitude.</u> London: HarperColins, 1994

To order log on to:
www.peterconsterdine.com

GEOFF THOMPSON *books*

Visit our website at www.geoffthompson.com

The Elephant and the Twig
The Art of Positive Thinking
14 Golden Rules to Success and Happiness

NATIONAL BEST SELLER

Have you ever heard the story of The Elephant and The Twig? In India they train obedience in young elephants (to stop them from escaping) by tying them to a huge immovable object, like a tree, when they are still very young. The tree is so large that no matter how hard the baby elephant pulls and tugs it cannot break free. This develops what is known as 'learned helplessness' in the creature. After trying so hard and for so long to break the hold, only to be thwarted time and again, it eventually believes that, no matter what it does, it cannot escape. Ultimately, as a fully-grown adult weighing several tons, they can tie it to a twig and it won't escape, in fact it won't even try.

Do you ever feel like this? That you are tied to an immovable object and can't break free? That you couldn't possibly give that presentation at work, that you would never be able to go it alone in business, or that you have to remain stuck in a social and lifestyle rut as there is no other alternative? This book shows you that, when it comes down to it, what ties you and prevents you from realising your potential is only a 'twig'. Geoff Thompson, renowned martial artist and author of Watch My Back guides you through the process of breaking the negative thinking that binds us all and helps you to take the plunge and properly take on life.

The Great Escape
The 10 Secrets to Loving Your Life
and Living Your Dreams

HARDBACK

If you feel Imprisoned in your job, a relationship or even worse if you feel trapped in your life then this book - the sequel to <u>The Elephant and the Twig</u> by best selling author Geoff Thompson is definitely for you. It offers the ten secrets to loving your life and living your dreams and helps you make The Great Escape from where you are to where you would love to be. You can be anything , you can do anything and you can go anywhere. You are a creator with the magic to create whatever you want from your short stay on this spinning planet, but there is a process that must be observed and a path to follow; this book unveils the secrets to both. But be careful, don't pick up this book unless you are ready to succeed, because once you have read the 10 secrets there will be nothing standing between you and your wildest dreams.

HARDBACK